Chasing Names on Nameless Water

Chasing Names on Nameless Water

Poems by

Ken Meisel

© 2025 Ken Meisel. All rights reserved.
This material may not be reproduced in any form, published,
reprinted, recorded, performed, broadcast,
rewritten, or redistributed without
the explicit permission of Ken Meisel.
All such actions are strictly prohibited by law.

Cover design by Shay Culligan
Cover image by Tim Marshall on Unsplash
Author photo by Anita Scott-Meisel

ISBN: 978-1-63980-900-4

Kelsay Books
502 South 1040 East, A-119
American Fork, Utah 84003
Kelsaybooks.com

*for Russell Thorburn, poet, music aficionado,
ally, friend*

Also by Ken Meisel

Sometimes the Wind (2002)
Before Exiting (2006)
Just Listening (2007)
Beautiful Rust (2009)
Scrap Metal Mantra Poems (2013)
The Drunken Sweetheart at My Door (2015)
Mortal Lullabies (2018)
Our Common Souls: New & Selected Poems of Detroit (2020)
Studies Inside the Consent of a Distance (2022)
The Light Most Glad of All (2023)

Acknowledgments

Thank you to the following publications, where versions of these poems previously appeared:

12 Mile Review: "Jasmine"
Amethyst Review: "Mary Magdalene Utters Words of Wisdom"
The Big Windows Review: "Listening to Astral Weeks & Emailing Russell Thorburn"
Book of Matches Literary Journal: "12 Quick Soliloquies on Identity & Truth"
Concho River Review: "St. Teresa of the Woods," "The Angel of Reverie Marks My Palms w/ Stars," "The Angel of Let Me Remember My Name"
Crab Creek Review: "Glory & Shame Cannot Be Separated from Each Other"
Cream City Review: "Watching Jo Jo Dance at the Sunset Strip"
Freshwater: "Under Water"
The Glacier: "Interview"
Hope Anthology: "We Are All God's Poems #1"
I-70 Review: "Youth," "Betrothal," "We Are All God's Poems #2," "First Kiss"
Lake Effect: "Under God (The Angels Discuss Our Music)," "St. Chopin of the Vacant Buildings," "The Angel of the I Is Elsewhere Speaks Straight Dope to Me," "Poem w/ Anguish in It"
Otis Nebula: "The Angel of Strange Loops / Rumbles Me Awake"
Panoply: A Literary Zine: "Mizocz Ghetto, October, 1942"
Peninsula Poets: "Anthony's Moss Piglet Water Bear"
Pirene's Fountain: "This Dream's on Me"
Rabid Oak: "Shock"
Rattle: "Reminiscences"
Reservoir Road Literary Review: "The Algiers Motel Incident, 1967 & Everything Else Thereafter Till Now"
San Pedro River Review: "Contemplation on Middle Age"
This/That/Lit: "My Horoscope in a Style of Harry Houdini," "The Caretaking Angels Encounter Me"
Tipton Poetry Journal: "The Obscure Darkness of Inanimate Things"
Trampoline: "Poem w/ Vengeance & Love in It"

U City Review: "St. William at the Artist Studio," "Some Cows & Angels Talking to Me," "Poem w/ the Color of Television Snow Inside It," "Contemplation on Dissonance," "The Recording Angel & The Angel of History (an email fragment)," "J, an Elegy in 20 Lines," "Chasing Names on Nameless Water"

Special thank you to *Lake Effect* for nominating "Under God (The Angels Discuss Our Music)" and "The Angel of the I Is Elsewhere Speaks Straight Dope to Me" for a Pushcart Prize.

Contents

Author's Note

I. Six Reflections on Violence

Mizocz Ghetto, October, 1942	19
Reminiscences	25
Watching Jo Jo Dance, at the Sunset Strip	28
The Algiers Motel Incident, 1967 & Everything Else Thereafter Till Now	31
Jasmine	34
Poem w/ Vengeance & Love in It	37

II. Illuminations: A Sequence on Youth, Life, & Stories We Tell to Our Future

1. Shock	41
2. Youth	43
3. First Kiss	45
4. The Angel of Reverie Marks My Palm w/ Stars	46
5. Marie	52
6. This Dream's on Me	54
7. Glory & Shame Cannot Be Separated from Each Other	55
8. Adelaide: at Her Mother's Final Burial	61
9. The Caretaking Angels Encounter Me	62
10. The Angel of Strange Loops / Rumbles Me Awake	65

III. Shape-Shifting: The Art of Changing the Picture Inside the Frame

Twelve Quick Soliloquies on Identity & Truth	71
St. Teresa of the Woods	75
My Horoscope in a Style of Harry Houdini	78
St. William of the Artists Studio	80

St. Chopin of the Vacant Buildings	82
The Angel of the I Is Elsewhere Speaks Straight Dope to Me	85
Poem w/ the Color of Television Snow Inside It	88
Betrothal	92
Anthony's Moss Piglet Water Bear	93
The Angel of Let Me Remember My Name	94
The Obscure Darkness of Inanimate Things	96

IV. Contemplations: Chasing Names on Nameless Water

Poem with Anguish in It	101
Contemplation on Middle Age	104
Contemplation on Dissonance	106
J, an Elegy in 20 Lines	109
Some Cows & Angels Talking to Me	110
An Elegy for Robert Wachler	114
We Are All God's Poems #1	118
The Recording Angel & The Angel of History (an email fragment)	119
We Are All God's Poems #2	123
Interview	124
Chasing Names on Nameless Water	126
Epilogue ('Round This Lover's Ring So Eternal)	128
Mary Magdalene Utters Words of Wisdom	130
Listening to Astral Weeks & Emailing Russell Thorburn	132
Under Water	133
Under God (The Angels Discuss Our Music)	134

Notes

"After a while he said if there's no bottom in your eyes, they hold more"

—Flannery O'Connor, *Wise Blood*

Author's Note

These poems are, at heart, meditations on identity and how it is unfixed, malleable, and, in the Buddhist sense, an illusion.

They begin in the horrific density of violence and what it aims to teach us—namely, that violence is the expression of a misanthropic ignorance towards the momentousness mystery of human life, death, innocence, and beauty.

And because identity—in lived practicum—is just the opportunity of the human self trying to awaken within the ineffable, other poems here play with the notion that the self is a practiced costume; and further, that *costume* is actually where spirit stretches and widens within form in order to identify a deeper playground of freedom—namely, the excited, unencumbered malleable shapelessness that we truly are—especially within moments of deep love, surrender, reverie, risk, loss, death, and beauty.

Finally, some of the culminative poems in this collection grapple with separation—through loss and death and apotheosis—as the reconciliation with impermanence that we require for wisdom's account with us.

—Ken Meisel

I.
Six Reflections on Violence

"You cannot fix what you will not face"

—James Baldwin

Mizocz Ghetto, October, 1942

"I'm thinking of collapse, of black winds' plunder"
—Forugh Farrokhzad

On the upper ridge, they were instructed to strip naked,
& then walk slowly over the crest of the mud hill

& then descend into the cold ravine & they were told
to lie still. & it was October, 1942, in the Mizocz Ghetto.

& one of the policemen, armed with a rifle, had sat still
at his breakfast table &, with a butter knife, spread

the jam across the dry toast &, spreading it red
over the crust, he paused, heard a shout outside to *hurry up,*

& so he gulped his black coffee, quickly ate the toast,
& he pulled his black boots on & also his officer's cap

& he joined his comrade, both armed, so they could
line the women up & tell them to strip naked in the chilled

October air. & some of the women were pregnant,
& some had babies wrapped in arms, everyone shivering.

Some might have read Ovid, or Rilke, while others
knew the exact way to make a perfect raspberry jam

or a bread that rose in a splendid oval before it baked
in an oven, on an all-day snowfall, for the family's meal.

& scattered above them, across the ridge, the women's
simple garments—robes, blankets, slips & autumn coats—

lay in random, hapless heaps while an irritant wind
chilled their naked bodies so that small goose bumps rose.

& the one officer, upon ordering them to strip naked to
nothing, said nothing other than what he could instruct,

which was simple, muted & direct, & it was enforced
occasionally by a quick shove of the barrel of the gun

forward, instructional, into the blunt, miserly October air
where, above, the sun had shrouded itself in an elevation

of high, bleak clouds. & because the culture of men always
appoints one man to be the superior of another, the older

officer grunted to the younger officer—the one who'd eaten
toast & jam & gulped a mug of coffee without cream or sugar—

to make sure the women stood in a straight, orderly line
as they dropped their garments, like pieces of angel wings,

to the dried, angry earth. & then the crueler, older policeman
grunted as he pushed his rifle muzzle forward—toward

the upper slope of the lethargic hill—& then he directed
the younger officer to herd the women up into the

creases of the concave ravine so that they could lay there,
half-wrapped like white flower petals over each other

& not be able to run away unless they ran upward, like
easy targets, or downward, so that, in their panic, they

might trip over other bodies lying subservient there,
obedient & frightened and subjugated with that fear that has

no name to it because it is wordless & it is unsparing, &
the older officer ordered the younger to shoot them all dead.

& this was an October morning slaughter of Jewish women
& their children, by German officers in the Mizocz ghetto.

& I have to tell about it, because violence is continuant.
& it is administrative & it is mechanical & it's routine, & it

is as alive as the women, laying meditative on that hill.
& when I look again at them, I see they are of all ages.

& in the first picture, they line up hesitantly, but obedient,
while the policemen herd them forward, with rifles.

& it is the first picture where I first notice a woman—
a beautiful, captive woman with shrieking, lovely eyes

& she is standing in line with all the other ghetto women
& it is her that I notice, because she is captive & upset,

& maybe has someone close on her mind, a lover. & I
notice her as *one*, distinct among the others. & I see, too,

many of the women & what it is they're doing. & I have
to tell you what it is, on this their last day, they're doing.

They are snuggling up to one another, as if in a shower line.
& in the *other* picture, they spoon one another, in death.

Others I see are perhaps twelve or thirteen, & brand new,
having had their first blood. & they are shy, alert,

watchful as girls of that age will be, & maybe an older one
is a mother, with an oldest son in the war, far off

on another ridge-sprawl of injured, bullet-blasted hill,
& he's trying to recall what he's been taught: how to kill

or survive for the sake of the next receding of light.
& maybe he is twenty & afraid of what might happen

to his young, Ukrainian fiancé . . . & maybe he's felt the tiny
oval picture of her, there in his jacket, before rubbing

the cold off his hands. & maybe I can *see* the young fiancé
there in this other picture. & she's dark-eyed & sensual,

& I've already found her in the first photograph of women
lining up & readying themselves to be exterminated.

& she's burying half her cheek into the hair of a woman
standing in front of her there. & maybe she's thinking

of the man who loves her . . . & how doubt is agnostic but *love*—
because it is hallucination—is faithful & holy & it's eternal.

& because I see her in the first picture, so alive, just before
she is slaughtered, I want now so bad to see her in the *other*

terrible picture where all the obedient women, stretched out
on their bellies as they are being murdered, lay still. & it is

because I don't want her to become *dead,* but, when I look
for her, I can't find her there because all the women are laying

face down, or rolled over on their unattended sides, & one of them
lays face up, gone, I suppose. It's not *her* & it's not pornographic:

she's just *done*. & it isn't horrible quite yet, because some of the
women are still alive, & they're watching & waiting & maybe

praying . . . & it doesn't become horrible until the duller, robotic
officer starts shooting at their bodies like they're a pile of white worms.

& when I look at them all laying here, so obedient & silent
& stretched together on their naked, secluded stomachs—

like moon-white angel beings awaiting their annihilation—
they look almost serene, tranquil, just like they are feeling

each other's purity . . . & maybe they feel the life in each other's wombs,
although some tuck & bury themselves in protective heaps

& I can't tell if they've been shot, or if they just demonstrate
an authentic rehearsal of it—while others stretch dormant

on their bellies as if sleeping & still others—young, old—
lay in the cold creases of earth, up-hill, trying to crawl away . . .

& I'm still looking for the woman with the shrieking eyes
because she's got to still be alive, prepping for her wedding,

& violence—this gross articulation of it—is mainly created
by men who have no comprehension of the *gift* death *gives* to us . . .

and therefore they cannot hold true to themselves autonomous love,
nor understand death's honor, and so they dwell in a trance voice . . .

& it is a nomadic voice, & it is a hard tumescent signaling,
& it is disreputable & it is unrepentant because it never

asks first if it is okay to shoot the whiteness of a body
or any other body-color because the explosive stain of red—

so horrid & spreading like a lunatic's flower across a naked
back, or on the opened breast or in the crucified naked palm,

or on the vulnerable buttocks or across the backs of smooth
shaven legs or risen, elegant cheeks—is *why* it exists

& why it is pandemoniacal & with us always . . . & that is why
it won't ever leave us . . . because it is acclaimed, it's celebrated . . .

& it's that fiancé I'm still trying to find in this murderous photo.
& I can't find her in the slaughter-pile . . . & I can't find her,

even when I run my eyes over every woman murdered there—
stretched dispassive & dead over one another like mermaids—

& so I turn the other photograph over in my hand, turn it over
& over again so that maybe I can call out loud to her & try to stop

her from walking in that horrified line . . . & it is the anguished
shrieking of her lovely, so afraid mouth that makes me know

that I cannot ever stop—even if by love or by a sad, fulsome
dismissal of it—*her killing* . . . & there is no end to it, this perfect

way she gently snuggles the woman in front of her, maybe
to offer, or to simply receive a friend's softness before death,

or maybe to feel, just one more time, the body's trusted warmth.
& there's no end to how it is women—no matter—practice an ethics

of care . . . & I can't figure out whether the boy, her groom-to-be,
ever finds out how she dies . . . & so I am telling him right now

that she died caring, caring like daughter of Heaven—
& with a civility, a grace & a bravery, & she is safe now

& she is with whomever wipes away the horrid red stains
from a murdered body in order to cleanse it from all that violence

so that what was once there, so very pure, always is—
& so that if he looks for her he will indeed find her

before all this horror happened,
& just as she was, with those bright so alive eyes.

Reminiscences

—Freud speaking with Breuer, in Lower Manhattan, NYC, September, 2001

I

They'd completed their rounds of patients at the hospital
and walked through the damaged city for about one hour,

before returning back to the clinic. "All the world's psychological traumas
can't be resolved by the Talking Cure—" Breuer said to Freud

as they strolled past the railway of the Hudson River where a man, drunk
on yellow bullets, *Nembutal,* rocked back

and forth like a Bedouin, a crazed orphan. The park was full
of young mothers and children, and the restless river,

punctured with refuse from the recent terrorist attacks,
glistened with floating glassware and plastic. Scrap wood

and debris rippled lazily over the sordid currents, and above them, swallows
from a bombed-out brownstone up the hill

rose and fell in haphazard, drunken reenactments. Someone played
a saxophone under a tree, and a boy, his thin mouth

full of lipstick, his face painted in clown, did silent mime
like a fragile doll. The media had issued warnings about toxic

debris in lower Manhattan, and the police warned of other, possible
terrorist attacks, and that citizens in all parts of the city

should maintain a calm alertness, wherever they went. The two medical
doctors paused, fed the ducks at the river's edge

of the park, and bought two cups of coffee for themselves,
before proceeding across the busy streets of New York.

II

"Oh, let me tell you of the woman I spoke with yesterday,"
Breuer said to Freud, nudging the latter on the elbow

as they walked beyond the park onto the street where the crippled clubs
hosted dinner music. "The woman had spoken to me

with specific complaints of losing the smile on her face, that it had been
torn off, really, after the tragic unfortunate death of her child,

just a boy—a sixteen-year-old boy with Sunnah caps and piercings—
by suicide, by leaping, she said to me, recklessly from an overpass

north of here and high on hallucinogens and too much Metallica."
"And that he'd been obsessively viewing socio-political material

about the East-West divide in our world, on the internet,"
Breuer added, while pulling out a cigar, "and that his mother

couldn't *stop* him from the torment of his obsessions."
And Freud, responding to Breuer, said, "oh *that* woman—

I saw her shaking quietly on a hospital bench, her little nose bleeding, her
small mouth torn in half like red leafy lettuce.

That's what she said to me, 'my torn mouth like red leaf lettuce,' "
Freud said to Breuer, shaking his head back and forth

like a pondering clock. "*Her* father suicided, *right?*" "And she
was of 'mixed blood,' *yes—?* She was part East-part West, *all of it,*

and so was her boy, isn't that right—? Wasn't he a product of Islam
and Reebox, of the maelstrom of religion and capitalistic imagery,

and of love and divorce, one of those children hopelessly divided—?"
asked Freud, and Breuer, aware of it, "yes."

III

"The present is a reenactment of history," Freud said, pondering
the piles of ash throughout the area, and Breuer, seeing this,

reached out, touched Freud's shoulder, said, "too bad about
the brownstone buildings that were demolished in the attacks,

and also about the ruined hopes for human peace."
And the sun, setting behind them, froze in their mouths

for a second, then burned. All of Manhattan glowed
in dusk's frontier.

Turned a curious mustard yellow like the air was salted, singed,
was aluminum threading, molded in disaster and chemical fire.

IV

"Do you think the world will ever be the same?" Breuer
absently asked Freud, "Do you think we will ever resolve

the factual elements of our experience?" They walked on,
passing the Trade Center's crumbled debris.

Pigeons rose from a bronze lamppost that had collapsed
in a pile of rubble.

"*No* I don't think we shall ever be the same," Freud answered. *Not ever.*
"The origin of *Hysteria Trauma*," said Freud

to Breuer, the both of them strolling along the frenetic grounds
of The Roosevelt Hospital now, "is one of inescapable shock."

And Breuer to Freud, "Hysterics, *all of us,* suffer mainly
from *reminiscences.* And reminiscence is the inevitable longing

for what's been before, and for what can never be the same again."
"It's the perfect mix of nostalgia and mourning,

our strange dilemma." "No talking cure can ever cure it,"
he said.

Watching Jo Jo Dance, at the Sunset Strip

Pain is the answer to the question *what about me.*

So you watch her, this exotic dancer in symbiotic pose
with the metal post running down from the ceiling . . .
at the point where the ceiling meets the *Sky*, this *Heaven*—
which is made partly of the mixture of human grit
and smog sitting like a dirty veil, high above the grease
and grime of Detroit City, on this early autumn evening
where the sky's blustery and gray, and it's engorged, and choked
with the smoke of factory spurts and cross-town traffic,
and the blanched winds of one season being absorbed,
head first, into another season's mouth. And where all the dead,
all the fallen angels, the jinns, the floating winged cloud bursts
of all the previous women, all of them killed or stolen
or mutilated, lean together, head-to-head like eager faces
hidden behind the stage door, cloaked now in shadow
like a cheeky chorus of dancers watching one more sister
run her leg up and down a pole as if to awaken it,
or herself, or herself *in it*—within the substance within the pole
which will give her her daily bread, her significance,
this life her father promised her, because it was his duty to.

All the women who dance are absorbed back inside the smoke.

The smoke is the *curtain,* dividing the civilization from the *civil.*

~

When a man strikes a woman, the curtain ripples, one more
apple falls out of the wounded fabric, a girl is born wrongly,
she falls and rolls across the linoleum floor, stopping, spinning
bumping up against the cupboards, or the floor boards,
or the doggy dish,
and the mother and father join hands to squeeze her into birth.

If this is wrong logic, tell me where the joy invades . . .
How it is the squiggling worm escapes the punctured apple,
and the princess bride is born, a whirling dervish, a Venus . . .

And look here, reader, at this muddy little angel of undaunted causes
standing as a companion alongside the little girl—so appointed—

the both of them, angel and child, squatting there beside the
doggie dish, and the spool of charcoal string that's wound firmly
around the little girl's fingers, tying her tight to this one
spectacular life.

~

Jo Jo's going to suck a sex toy now. It's in her mouth.
No matter what she's doing, all is focused on what she'll
take inside her opened mouth.

The mouth—because it's a physical cavity where melody sits,
melody, of course, being the strings of the spirit singing
what it is that differs within it, within the body—knows
only the law of incorporation and expulsion, all of that,
and so this woman, this dancer, is fellating a banana and a sex
toy, both, because it is legal, and true to do so, sex being
the mouth's prerogative, like the hand, and anus, and all the
rest, too.

And for this the men, sitting under the stage lights
laugh out loud and clap, and throw dollar bills at her pumps.

There is no end or beginning to the question one asks
of oneself at the start of something truly big—like sucking on
a sex toy in public, at a bar called the Sunset Strip in Detroit
which is, of course an oxymoron, because there is no sunset
on Michigan Avenue in Detroit worthy of that kind
of naming—because asking the question itself is a type
of concealing, because nobody can tell that kind of story
rightly, the story of why a woman will suck on a banana or a sex
toy in public, at a strip club called the Sunset Strip.

Okay, I'll try to translate her smile . . . here's what it says:

Telling the truth of why I suck on a sex toy is a kind of concealing.
The mouth says it best, which is, I suck to hide *why* it is I suck . . .

All the right answers are inside the curtain which separates the civilians
from the civilization doing all this promoting and all this wounding . . .
It is as if the curtain catches all that aggresses, falls, is ruined . . .

Maybe that's why the fallen angel is enjoyed the best in the West.

Pain is the answer to the question *what about me* . . .

Later, afterwards, standing outside the club where there's been
a fight—between men competing for a parking spot—she asks me
while lighting a cigarette if what she does is right or wrong,
and I see the smile flying off her face like a line of Morse Code
concealing something caught between competing versions of herself . . .

The *versions,* being of course, the self, and the self within the self . . .

Pain is the dancer spinning there on the stage between the self
and the other self. It knows no conscience—because the men absorb it.

The Algiers Motel Incident, 1967 & Everything Else Thereafter Till Now

Up Woodward Avenue, as the fires around us
rage like adrenalized orange lilies—some of the lilies
blooming out of the apartment building windows,
while others devolve into furnaces in the parked cars
now imploding in on themselves in cavernous flames
from the Everything, steeping itself right back down
into the Nothing—he and I walk together. He is
describing the style of conversation at play here:
is saying: *the whole city is Molotov cocktails and looting,*
is gunshots, wounds and shouting, is bloodshed,
and a style of thirst, something always unrequited;
and he tells me: *this is how you all commune here together,*
as if violence, *atrocity,* is a language. A communal
experience. Says to me: you won't understand it—
unless I draw it for you as an Angel; let's call it the
Angel of Atrocity—some avenging being, come
here to advertise itself as a form of mayhem and horror.
It could happen in Detroit or Portland. Does it matter?
You see, it's so very hard to tolerate the stupefied *gasp*
emerging from our differences here, and so we must
flood it full of these torrents of atrocity, because we
hate what we cannot know and we crave what appeals
to us—which is how this wheel turns on and on.
We walk together up the avenue where fires burn. He
shows me where the Algiers is. *What is the Algiers Motel?*
I ask, and he informs me it is just a party den, where
some young black musicians and some white girls
are drinking together, and shooting the shit, and he
shows me one of the men, embracing a girl, and he says,
there it is: *this thirst?* and it is okay; it is the way
we design a fixed containment: the man is excited
for the way her skinny languorous body embraces
his body, and she too, is *a doubt,* seeking to fix herself
to *a surety,* which is how we all confuse a fulfillment
of desire with *being something;* some finite object
of attraction—in a whirlpool of not-knowing. And now

he shows me how the crazed policemen will arrive,
themselves also fixities inside a blue uniformed style—
seeking to gain egress against oblivion, and so they
must *be something,* some *aggregate* against all this existence
and so we must watch how they line the scared white
women and the black men up against the wall—so
as to locate where it is the impulse to *play together*
becomes a *locomotion of sin,* or a broken rule none
of them can comprehend. It is okay to *watch* this, says
the Angel of Atrocity: we are just noticing with our
craving and our thirst how it comes to be we enter
into aversion with one another: but let me shift your
focus, he says: now look *down*—at the fluoride blue
swimming pool, where they were swimming together;
check out the diseased palm tree there, in the center
of Detroit City! And notice the rear annex, where people
gather together in the kitchenettes to cook food, gulp
their handfuls of drugs in a circle. *It's just life,* he says.
They're just attempting to release themselves—from a
fullness, that's all. And it is this fullness, this *satiety,*
this deep craving to satisfy what is astonished alarm
that stumbles us down into mayhem, into atrocity.
And now he has me touch my own belly where I am
numb; he tells me: look, you cannot fill up horror
with this false emptiness; you must *own* what you are.
We are confused actors; we must see what we do.
Only then will we be able to cease injuring ourselves.
This is just one incident; to be followed by everything else.
I tell you, there is no end to how cruelty plays chess.
Racism, greed, rabid ignorance; these are the atrocities.
Now he shows me the policemen shooting the kids.
Shows me how they are gunned down in the motel.
We watch them collapse into their own piles of atrocity.
Points to the policemen who are doing all the killing.
Tells me *they're drowning in oblivion*, because to be free
is too heavy for them, and so they shoot *it* dead, all
this free space to expand. They are constricting, so as to
create a world more governable for themselves—

the riddle of this mandala, being confused virtues:
this rage, this terror, this crazed *defense* of territory.
And it is this *catastrophe* that shows us—again—that we
are already a broken territory that doesn't even know
it is already broken. And so one of the policemen seeks
himself inside aggressive strivings while the other
seeks himself inside assimilation of disorder, and *you,*
says the Angel of Atrocity, to *me,* seek yourself in the
fantasy that all this we are seeing can be computable
within an abiding sense of self, which is untrue, but
you persist in it; in this torment of sickness that tells
you the external (this motel) and the internal (you),
are *distinct* thirsts that you will have to make sense of,
because you too are a matter of history on the wheel.
Morality's always earned by an accumulation of hurt,
by a horrified destruction of the body, a mangling of it—
which is why the imago of George Floyd stings us now
and why the Algiers Motel is one of the cauldrons of hell,
like a story of understanding that cannot understand itself,
he whispers; and ethics measures the care or misuse
of the truth, which is why consent always mattered.
Tells me it is okay: because bare attention to detail
is all we have in the face of atrocity, all we're capable
of doing in the open ignorance of all this clinging
and hurt calamity. And then he embraces me gently,
holds me while I vanish into the Algiers Motel incident,
and into everything else thereafter, till now.

Jasmine

After I tell you this, you'll understand why it is
our brains are maps.

Jasmine's nine years old, right hand stuffed
with crayons, a red, a purple,

a gray, an orange, and her left hand's just
gripped a ragged sheet of print paper,

two other sheets, smothering her
muddy, untied summertime shoes

and her eyes are cliffhanger histrionics,
they're little globes of echo-fire

and she's absentminded and delirious
as she scrawls a picture of a little girl

tied down into a chair—the girl's almost glued to it—
and over her, a mom—two insane pigtails

screaming out of the back of her adult head—
is sprawled all over little Jasmine

like a shadow and—wait for it—this is
the map-making part I'd wanted to tell you—

the monster-mom holds a thin cigarette
in her claw-like hand and she's

burning holes in the little girl's cheeks.
I didn't want to tell you this.

It made me sick to see it.
My stomach, a sudden epicenter of illness.

My education, like broken Easter eggs
dried up in an attic's corner.

It's dusk when Jasmine draw-scrawls it
for us and, up and down the sides

of the piece of paper—just like a border,
amazingly—are flames of barn fire

and a cross-fade of smoke clouds
descending over the two peoples' heads,

as if drugging them both, putting them to sleep.
I am a dwelling, that's for sure.

And Jasmine's in my abode and I am in hers.
And what we do with this abode

can only be determined by my response to it.
We are a give-and-take system.

No map advances any other way.
And so when she stops, when she shoves

the drawing at me, she has no interest
in telling me anything about it

except to point out to me the exact way that
orange—like an assignment of coloration—

burns a spot on a little brown face that,
when I look closely at it, has no eyes on it

except curdled pointed dots, tinctures of spirit,
and her hands, depicted in the picture,

hang limp like sunflowers, like lost fins.
And the monster-mother is cosmopolitan,

a whole globe of effigial earth, a foreshock,
and suddenly Jasmine's electric, she's

hurling herself against my chair like she's
part demiurge, part earth-quake,

and that's because maps are tectonic,
and they are rubbed events, impingements

that seek egress, that break locked points
open, whether we like it or not.

And she's twisting me around in the chair.
She's tapping me on my cheeks.

She's jumping up and down, like she's
waiting for something to happen.

She's on my lap in a ball now,
and these are the maps we live by.

Poem w/ Vengeance & Love in It

After the police arrived, muscled folks away,
the sweetness happened. I'll get to that later.

In those days the gray sky was pulpy, & the sad trees
were disfigured, grotesque, & the bars, along the street,
were unafraid & that was why men fought
until they were misshapen, ugly, like vegetables,
& the jukeboxes, momentous, blasted on
until all the violence, like music, softened, petered out,
& someone would stumble out the door, whistling
"You're All I Need," or "Chasing Rainbows."
& someone big, a man in a cap would fling his arm
over another man, like comrades & they'd lumber
off to a parked car around the corner, laughing it
all off.

    &

I'll tell you one more secret: they loved each other,
the men there who worked by day, alongside
each other as pipe fitters, as carpenters, as painters,
& the fights were just disgracious, unjustified
expressions of that wordlessness in them,
that's all, & that's all you need to know.

    &

this was when we were alone, in a room.
He stripped his shirt off, dense with sweat
& somebody's blood & his eyes thick with
tears.

& I held him as he cried, & it was too late.
& I poured him strong coffee & we sat,
two men, alone as two far-off stars a mile
into each other's light beam & all the dark
between them, on them, cavernous, but usual.

& when two men cry against an impotence,
when they punch with a vengeance
until they bleed, people move away, they flee,
& it's just the rage of not knowing something yet,

& people get scared of it, they call the police
& it's because men's violence is veiled & inborn.

& that's why one throws stars against a ceiling
while the other hurls rocks against a face
& here's the softer part: men feel a vague
self-hatred until somebody tells them they
are beautiful &, when that happens, usually
when they are laying still in a bed, a leg
curled under a sheet & a lover there so struck
by the languid beauty of it, tells him, "you, sir,
are as beautiful as a streak of summer honey,"
most men long to hear it but they can't, or
won't, because they are indefinite, & undecided
as to what they are

    & here's the sweeter part:
when I told him his life was a worthy root tuber,
something dug deep & rooted in dirt &, yet,

clear & luminous, & with white skin trying
with all its might to be in the light of a day
without all the self-hatred, he put his head
in his large, wounded hands & cried until the

coffee pot interrupted us & he stood up, said,
"enough." & later, when we saw one another

at the Flame Restaurant, him, stirring through
oatmeal & me, sipping a coffee & reading
Camus' Essays, he didn't say anything to me.

He just smiled, grinned deep down. Indeed.

II.
Illuminations: A Sequence on Youth, Life, & Stories We Tell to Our Future

"Following the stately and rapid ship,
in the wake following."

—Walt Whitman, "After the Sea Ship"

1. Shock

A day, long ago, when you saw

the wind menace down from

a culvert's high side
—in the Blue Ridge Mountains—

and rip and shred your tent
like an invisible beaked bird, aggressing against it.

You stood shell-shocked,
watching the violence of it all. A beer in hand.

Was it God, or Great Spirit?
Some advance of bad luck like a fortune
teller's omen, laid down in the cards?

Something that makes the Universe like a portent?

Should you have known this? The remembrance—
of other shocks, kept camp-side like a book?

The self must be a fabric of old holes.
Shock points that puncture its ignorant solidity.

Portals too, made of weird exits and entries.

You'd been drinking, but what does that matter?
You were also reading Travels With Charley

by John Steinbeck. Weren't you prepared?

The whole side of your tent

went soaring down—merciless—
into a tangled landscape made of laurel.

Proving—what? That beauty too
is a dark, hungry hole? Something thirsty?

Or that this kind percussive *consequence*
is just the arbitrary design point

of the self's gradual assistance—

an assistance slapped awake by shock episodes—

into a greater wisdom:

a wisdom born of kickback and chaos?

Things tear apart, even when you
plan for necessary shelter.

After that, you slept in your car.

2. Youth

Youth, you know, is the very first cup
of wealth and loss. Of how thievery gets its due.

Do we ever get over it—how we're stolen from?
The prettiest girl, her legs gone to

mangled roots in the sudden car accident,
and you boys, hushed, watching her

be lifted up from the cold wheelchair
by her mother, her older brother, herself.

So brave and so broken all at once.

How in a deep dream you saw an angel
or some sponsor tell you that we're made

in astonishment—over and over again—and it
fills us up with so much brevity and so much

light that we're comingled with everything,
and that's the only way we overcome theft.

All the pieces of life—a jig saw puzzle—
scattered to shards, over and over again.

We learn to live w / it & it humbles us.

Is that grief? The hand's careless swipe?
What is the hand that gives and takes?

Is it some form of sorcery? Some true aim
that derides us as it provides to us?

Nothing you get keeps you to it. Not quite.
Love, the most unfaithful angel, lets go.

Kneeling in the woods you found
the small stone circle where the campfire's

glow and halo rested for a few hours
before the late steaming night sky,

full of clouds and mysteries, smoked it.
The rest of the area, silent as sorrow.

The youthful kids, partying here, so absent—
their varied voices flung in wet echoes.

Even the beer bottles, left here to dry,
were muffled by a trapped smoke there.

You stood over it, studying how the smoke
—in swirl and vortex—roamed so angelic.

Something so wild and esoteric in the glass:
dark and yet swirling in a vibrant blue hue.

Not quite like our afterthoughts. More.

3. First Kiss

It wasn't the way the sky grew clouds in it like cattleya orchids,
nor the songs of the breezes, blowing wispy through the yews

against the brick side of the church, nor was it the feeling
in my stomach when she moved her lips like a small wet

avalanche across my own tender lips, nor was it the irresistible grace
of the divine little yellow flowers planted there in the garden

as they bent low in the aftermath of the summer rain, nor was it
the sheer excitement, shifting in intensity, as the rest of my body,

trembling like a chorus hearing her voice inside it, moved into her
body too, so that someone witnessing us might think we were

whispering, even mouthing something quite pure, some wholesome secret
into the life of another; and maybe even transferring it, like an irreducible

beauty, from one lover's kiss igniting across the lips onto another's
so that the world closed a door, just so that we could exist in that

moment and just for one another; *no,* listen: what it was beyond all of this
was that when she put my hand over her heart, my hand, a chosen

lover's card, just a square little playing card, and she whispered to me
that she'd waited for me by the door, so that she could study me walking

across the blacktop and humming to myself some old AM radio tune
made popular that summer, you see, between seeing and *not*

seeing, I was *realized;* I was made into a new boy by a pretty girl;
and this world, I learned, is dreams liberated from their sleep;

and a first kiss is a seizure of joy that comports straight to the soul
beyond a *first time;* and we are nothing if we are not born at all.

4. The Angel of Reverie Marks My Palm w/ Stars

In reverie the soul is being born was what she was whispering to me.
& in dying we are atoms to atoms just like when we are being born / &

it's so fine these divine imaginings . . . It's so corrective what they say to us
is what she was whispering to me at a sea-side bar; & isn't it like the moon

to masquerade as a woman with a mole (like an olive seed) on her cheek,
& isn't it lunar how it lights in her eyes, so that her face seems like eternity
       & her earrings shine like far away stars?

―――――

& I was talking over the ice that she shook in a cocktail mixer for me
when I whispered to her what Keats said in one of his letters

when he said, *we read fine things but never feel them to the full;
& the rough edge will fly immediately into a proper compactness* . . .

which must be the self, like a loaf of bread, baking to fullness,
to completeness, she answered me in after-thought, serving me the drink.

&, likewise, I remember myself at just thirteen years old

& I was standing alone in a person's living room & just trespassing there—
stealing all their bottles of home-made champagne & cooked food—
& that somehow, theft felt like a crime of hands, it was so easy to do,

it *was* an exactness in me becoming somehow furtive, fluid, alive and free
like never before
so that I could believe all growth starts first as inventive theft

    &—still later—

with a dew-eyed girl who smoked a joint with me & then let me
run my two fingers across her lips like they were the silken edges
      of a pink frangipani—
like some exact smoothness of eternity rounding the outer rim of her lips
so that my fingers could explore the edges of their beauty in bright pink
lip gloss—

       I felt it, again, this rough edge of proper compactness

softening into a fullness / into cream / & then / into an open border / . . .
into something so easy it felt like the breath of gravity kissed upon me . . .

---

so that later, broad-band, all the stolen champagne bottles held tight,
I could stand upright in a mirror and study myself at arms length

and then shame myself for the theft—the ignoble physicality of it—

while at the same time I could feel the glory of it marking me
as somehow Unknowable, Invincible, Elastic, almost Savage—
      Unbound, Disloyal, Masa Confusa, a Criminal—

& then I could feel myself to the full . . . & then empty myself out like
a vessel of fullness into the mirror's ovular vacancy . . . its eternity . . .

& I'd know, too, like never before, that we sometimes do in fact live out
of our bodies & way way out of our minds too / . . . & we're atoms to atoms

somehow being-us-born . . . . / & our thoughts of self, well, they *exposition*
    us—

our thoughts *situate*, they grow in such a manner that they actually *invent* us,

& we are thoughts we never thought we were— we're just masa confusa
picking out the hands that will steal us all we need to us.

& we're a flourish of words into the infinite; / we're names that choose us /
as much as we choose them for ourselves to become so utterly *costumed* in.

& so, we amalgamate; & we embody for a while what chooses us / yes we
do . . .
    & isn't that just the law of transmutation . . .?

. . . the woman—the bartender at the bar—asked me as she passed me
        the cocktail glass—it was a Reverse Manhattan—
she was interrupting me recalling me in a memory . . . her quizzical eyes,
blinking; & me, replying to her: *yes*, oh hell yes, it *is* transmutation . . .

&, while kissing that girl w/ the frangipani lips,

(—me, going into that deep youthful memory again—)
& just kissing my girlfriend's lip-glossed frangipani lips
while we were high on weed & listening to Jimi Hendrix
playing the Star Spangled Banner at Monterey Pop

I unpacked a towel, & in it, the bottle of cheap Champagne
        I'd stolen, & then we uncorked it, she & I,

& we sipped it like a valley of stars super-softening the furtive hearts
so revealed & alive in us / & we did it / while playing a record on a turntable

just so that we could express how innocent-afraid we were
to be revealed as one person in a role, in an identity /
        her, her as a girl, & me, / me as thirteen-year-old boy,

a thief, a Pied Piper, a champagne criminal, an innocent arrow
so fearful of where the bow & quiver could truly
        shoot me /

        & also

where it could land me at some point / . . . me, so captivated

by its flight that my bliss could be greater than its loft . . . / oh yes.

& my bliss /—all of it—
being the cosmic after-shoot of the arrow lofting oft-ward—
        where spirit leaves the bone / & is inhabited by another / *a girl* /

(this is what the angel of reverie, its face like an exploding sunflower
of light still being born, whispered to me

alone there in the afterwards / as the girl snuggled close to me & she slept /
(her head, laying softly across a mauve pillow
while the marijuana haze lingered above us like atomic clouds . . .)

& then I knew, once & for all, that I could be *inhabited,* could become
       anyone or anything at all . . . this is true.

———

& in reverie the soul is being born, is was what Jimi Hendrix's
       guitar wrote into the Monterey sky—

(look at it with me reader as you read this poem, smelling the cannabis)

       & the eyelids of the kids on the lawn there, super fogged in reverie,

while the tall buildings of the city behind it, shrouded in coastal mist-fog,
       metabolized into marijuana clouds . . .

&, in atoms-to-atoms, a secret part of me stenciled & spooned itself
       along the soft rim of her right hand as it curled above the pillow
       as she slept so completely there / . . . as she fell into the dream . . .

& some of me, / you know / I put it / *me* / into the soft psalm-like hymns
of her breath / as she inhaled & then exhaled there / so I could fully

       live out of my body / & inside *her* sleep / in *her* dreams / in *her* life

like I'd become a ladder losing all its steps to vapor & to ambiguity & to
lost ambit, which is love's transmuted, accelerated movement . . . yes.

& you know she, too, could melt vaporous right into *my* sleep, *my* locus . . .

———

but it's just today / becoming yesterday / dear boy / / / . . .
is what the sophisticated lady masquerading as the bartender

tells me as she serves me a new glass of bourbon, jiggling the ice there / . . .
       & it's just Time massaging the cells in your body. / & it is Time

massaging them because your soul is being reborn by reverie—oh yes it is,
       & by names awakening in mist / under wet fog / under high stars /

& by every act of recalling a person / *asleep* / *inside you* / forever alive . . .

& isn't that how we find ourselves again . . . as step ladders of light?
       (Atoms-to-atoms; & light vapor born anew in bodies / . . . in breath?

Erotics entering and dissolving the compact walls of a self's fixity—so that
we'll never know a proper, fixed exactness?)

Maybe we're a fixity that says we *cannot,* simply *cannot* become other,
but the law of Spirit says bullshit, we can . . . & sometimes, lovers, we must.

    (the angel of reverie smiling there)

        &,

isn't it because we're nothing other than a permeable membrane of skin
       masquerading as a two-legged form / . . . spiritualized / again?

        &

don't we just stand in a stripe of mirrored light, everyone entering us . . .?

Aren't we just a spiritualized reverie / being-us-born on a wheel of life . . .?

    & me, replying back to her: Yes. Yes. We are, in fact . . . *Yes.*

(Maybe I've confused you, reader, just now with all this metaphysical rap?)

    But I remember *exactly* what my girlfriend whispered to me

when she awoke from sleep. She said: "I felt your heartbeat in my legs.
    You were a two-wheeled bike of white swans pedaling into me . . ."

& who was I to argue what designates an anointed place in another?

Who was I to argue the depth of an otherness—her—living in me, now?

Even if I was a pair of swans pedaling thru her long legs & into her spirit.

    &,

she said, the soul is a lullaby an angel forgets, until we sing it in another.

&, besides, it was a good night to let somebody else
tell me I was in fact an angel

    disguised

as a thief / an arrow / a soul.

5. Marie

I don't think the tenor sax passages in any of those Dorsey songs
helped calm the evenings down when they fought.

No matter, he'd hurt on a bottle & she'd piss off on him.

Once, I heard her put "Yearning," or "East of the Sun"
on the turntable & I'd see them through the cracked

window pane, dancing it up, slow or fast, & she'd hug on him
like he was the side of a mountain

        &

you know love, for sentimental reasons, makes us
near-sighted & we lose our way

        &

she'd wail on him, afterwards, when he'd cheat on her with the barmaid
or the Laundromat girl or the counter keep at the 5 & dime

&, in December, when the chilled snow settled like froth ale
in the pine trees & the old cars on the street sunk low, into delirium,

I'd watch him hurl the snow with a shovel, over the fence
into the neighbor's yard, & the neighbor, a veteran, would

lumber outside in his bathrobe,
      threating war; & the two men

         would go at it, cussing, cursing,

& she'd shove the front door open, cookies in hand,
& she'd offer one to the neighbor; & he'd stop,

push past & climb the wood stairs for a bite,
& she's say to the both of them, "you wear me out,"

                        &

to be wasted at something, totally in it, is to act
in a vaudeville act, like a caricature, a fool

& "it's crazy, sometimes, what we could have had,"
she'd say to him, begging him anyway to hold

her tight to him. & she'd say, "I need this."

                        &

in the hot summers I'd hear them screwing & loving
something inadmissible in each of them. & finally,

to make a long story short, I never knew her name

until I watched him leave one morning in a suit coat,
his eyes dark & brooding & his hands,
                      purple, bruised in a bar fight,

&, at the curbside his brother was there, waiting
in a black Cadillac. & the two of them
                drove off,

I later learned, to the cemetery, & her name
                was Marie,

& she was the special arrangement of a song
he'd hummed once, before the war, before he knew

he'd find her at a hospital. & she was an aid.
& love, you know, is a deafness trying to hear a song

until the song begins at Nixon's Grand Theater, in 1937,
at least that's what he told me once, after
        a night of long-playing 78s & hard gin. Him just
staring into a bleak cup, stirring all that heartache.

6. This Dream's on Me

On the darkest part of the evenings, when the creek was low
& flooded with bugs & irritated slivers of water,

I'd park the car, crawl out of it, bottle in hand, & I'd
tell the trees "this dream's on me."

                                              &

"women never tell a lie they can't explain," he'd say
to me, suitcase in hand as he'd prep to fly to Cuba.

& that song, "Star Me Kitten," by REM, would
saturate the bar & we'd sit there, listening to it on the jukebox,

trying to forget the night & all its personal difficulties.

& in Cuba he'd curtail himself, shoot up in rooms
made of beige curtains & rough, cheap couches

& then he'd return; & I remember him telling me he'd hooked up
with a guitar player & a bongo group, & they did

Woody Herman's "Blues Downstairs," which was
difficult to explain & "nothing is going my way," he'd say

to me, late at night, receipts in his pocket, bleary-eyed

                                              &

some men never find the river, they never find a day
going their way & so they make time up, they pick

a day like a guitar string & they wile away the hours
until the years struggle hard to keep up. & a tire

falls off one day, just like a suit & tie, & that's it.

7. Glory & Shame Cannot Be Separated from Each Other

"examine the allegory as allegory"
—Milan Kundera

I don't remember if her face was blue or green in the neon lights,

or if she was coming off the speed, or on one more hit of it but, being

Desirable, she whispered to me, is only what other people consider
me to be, in their personalized fantasies, in their interior rooms—

& it's how we see, or don't see one another; & it's how we miss
the knot, the twisted heart of who we really are when night splits us,

& that is because the self—me—is just an oval with mascara lining it,
& we are merely the totality of gestures that others fantasize us to be . . .

& it makes me so very tired & so fucking sad, she said.

& she wiggled herself down to adjust the flayed strap
on her pearl-studded dancing pump

as the lights of the disco globe rollicked and ricocheted
to the thrum of backbeats, to all that aggressive drumming,
& she whispered to me to kindly *kiss* her mouth, then quit her fast,
so she could end the evening again by laying across her bed,

her ears wrapped in head phones, just to sleep. Just to forget desire.

———

The bottlebrush eucalyptus offered red pom-poms to the night
& when we shook it, drunk then & trying to end the night

by pushing immortality against it

my buddy, Bill, waved a pine stick at the bottlebrush eucalyptus

in a duel with it, to defeat it at the edge of the delinquent creek,
& he doused me with a beer. He hugged me.

This was two weeks later, & we were just messing about, up too late
in a night of drinking & revelry at a beach side bar
& trying to revive what could be discovered beyond the
edge of desire, which is a recklessness, seeking its end glory,

& it never ends the way you'd think it would end, something plunders the
night, & so he doused me again, to fits of laughter. & I

boldly pulled out the Whitman poem, "That Music Always Round Me,"
& I read the famous lines:

*that music always round me, unceasing, unbeginning, yet long untaught
I did not hear, but now the chorus I hear & am elated . . .*

with glad notes of daybreak I hear.

It saves my life when I read that, I said to Bill. It saves my life.

& Bill doused me again with beer. & we reveled to the songs of birds
finding their excited, hopeful wakefulness on the stretched telephone lines
& inside the soft-skirted serenade of bottlebrush trees.

———

Immortality is darkened by melancholy, that's its problem, she said.
No, *that melancholic nostalgia is just what we* paste *over it*, I said.

And she said, fuck off—laughing now—fuck off, Irish poet boy.

———

When she'd take her jewelry off—the pearls & earrings—& face herself
in a bathroom mirror to flare out the raven-black curls of her luscious hair,
to wave it across her wide shoulders like an irrational black sea,

she'd tell herself that her face was heavy & burdensome, & forgettable too
because she was Latina & of mixed blood, she was birthed in divided lines,

&, although her face was cut in a ragged, thirsty beauty, desperate like a flower opening & not really knowing it makes a difference—

&, because she actually looked like her enraged grandfather
when she flared her nostrils, especially when she was impassioned—

there was nothing I could say to convince her that the golden earrings
or the torn jean jacket she draped over her rich, succulent body,
or the keen intelligence she expressed in just a few cut open words

was enough of an argument to justify her personal worth or
her enriched beauty, & she'd scoff at me anyway—unrepentant, sly—
& she'd push me away from her in a half-laugh & she'd slug the drink again
& she'd scrub the rouge off her cheeks with a purple washcloth
& I'd run my hungry fingers over her reddened lips just to touch their
hot oil smile . . . & she'd whisper, *fuck off Irish poet boy,* kissing me . . .

& a rich, but succulent frozen warmth grew there as she grinned at me,
& she'd twist a crucifix, call herself a diva-bitch, & hug me, so glorified,

but some people are suicidal because they are fatigued
& defeated by an indescribable shame in them. & it's a stingy,
curdled, swollen kind of glorified thing & it never lets up—

& so there is nothing that the mirthful, ever joyous morning birds,
singing their lush melodies in the bottlebrush trees, can do.

―――

After Bill & I crashed the car, in downtown St. Petersburg,
we actually tried to gather up the windshield glass.

The tape deck was still pushing out Charley Parker. It must have been 5:30 am.

I think the end result has nothing to do with how we guess it.

It's more like a mangled embrace. &, besides, we were ridiculously

proud to have wrecked the car to boppin' good ol' Charley Parker,
& that justice was damn good enough of an outcome for us,

especially as we watched the sun rising like a buttercup tree
over the forget-me-not silver tone of the bay. So glad to be alive.

———

& to put it differently, I think we have a place in us that dooms us

& we go there whenever it pulls us to it, whenever we have to, you see,

& it's both shamed & glorified, & it's a doomed red eucalyptus

pom pom

capable of being bullied, torn asunder or battered by a stick,

& who *is* the invisible person in us when no one else persists?

How do we find that lost person when the spirit demands it?

She'd bawl me out when I'd argue these notions with her

& that's because we take good care of the doomed invisible in us
because it's a refuge in us, it's a weightless shadow, we praise it

& it keeps us company—it holds us when we are afraid to be alone

& also afraid to be *with* someone, to be rocked into comfort

so we can fall apart, be collapsed in the soft narcotic nuptials of night.
& that's because, sometimes, we are so terrified to be saved.

Fuck off, Irish poet boy she'd say, kissing me close. Pushing away.

———

Are we mangled by what embraces us? Every embrace factors a price.

She asked me: "why would you flap like a black bat inside my fucking rage?" Shuffled the coffee cups back from the table, to the cupboard.

Moved across the kitchen, laugh-raging like a bolt of black obsidian.

Gulped a few pills. Cranked the radio dial, *love lift us up where we belong.*

Wrapped a blanket round herself, pulled it down to expose her shoulder.

———

She walked the colors of the world across the room, dancing high on speed.

I watched her because I was trying to find where the lover is photographed

inside a mangled embrace, under a sky speckled with coyote stars. No moon

———

& people hurt themselves for death or for immortality, & that's because

it's a way to claim something for a paltry refuge of a self that withers.

"Glory & Shame cannot be separated from each other—"

is what Milan Kundera said in his book, *Immortality.*

"*I* feel, *therefore I am,* is the basis of the self," he said.

Glory & Shame act to cripple *me,* she argued back,

during a stroll on the beach—& it's a style of *descent,* spun

on the wings of death. *The tug-of-war I cling to, brings me.* She said.

& she was high on opiates when she said it. Drug-Embraced like a lover.

The dare to live happy always frees a prisoner of failed hopes, I said.

She let go of my hand then, mumbled, *Oh yes,* walked into the waves.

With finned hands, she fanned back the headlong shore-breaker waves

thudding against her sensuous hips. & with cupped palms, overturning

splashed stars, she swept the jeweled cosmos behind her. Sighed.

es una extraña magia fuerte ser invisible, incluso desde las estrellas, she

answered herself in Spanish. Giggled like someone I didn't know.

It's a strange strong magic to be invisible, even from the stars.

———

& for that fistful of a woman with lovesick eyes & a face like a fire,

I'd kiss

the stars igniting her face until the ocean's soft bed of waves

swept themselves into a chiffon glistening—

into a nightgown of coyote stars to clothe her body in—

& I'd sing a lullaby to her

until the sirens, fringed and bleeding, came.

8. Adelaide: at Her Mother's Final Burial

And when she grabbed in her little hand the rubber black spider

&

she lifted it across the funeral scene, above the plastic fire truck
& the metal station wagon that was the final hearse

that carried her mother, "her very very very dead mother in it—"
her very dead mother dangling like a collapsed liparsis orchid in it—

her mother's body made of purple paper, mind you,

&

petals smashed & spilling out of the windows so that the dead mother

resembled

someone who'd fallen injured, drunk or demolished, into the bed sheets
after too much drinking, or a stroke or a faint-spell, or, finally, *absence*—

& she attacked the hearse with the black spider, calling it—the spider—
cancer, cancer.

& she raised the spider over the stuffed animal world she'd created
to provide a family & a group of witnesses to all this,
& she touched every little animal lined up there, cursing, s*pider, cancer,*

& she was four years old when she said all this, declared it.

Her tight little angel hands gripping the murderous spider in them,
                         holding it over all that world of innocence,

& we buried her mother—her very completely vanquished mother

which was a bent purple orchid that drooped like a silenced impulse

into the pillowed, side-cushion of a green couch—

& she climbed up into my lap, her bright eyes blazing,
               & she asked me with her wide-open eyes & her innocent heart

          what playground in Heaven mothers, with cancer, go?

9. The Caretaking Angels Encounter Me

This was on a foggy winter morning, on the back streets of Venice Beach
where the meth addicts hid in messy cars and did their business

    while the city of Los Angeles

ticketed their junked cars for illegal parking.

I was standing alone under a strange tree, studying a lovely yellow flower's
pointed tips while the innocent children chased one another
across a play ground in a spirited game of hide-and-seek or rag tag—
    it was difficult to figure it out.

    Along Abbot Kinney Blvd
I watched an addict watching a woman as she passed quickly by him in her
    yoga pants—

she was chirping steadily on her cell phone to someone—
and some part of him began his initiatory descent into hell

while the muscle men on the wild beach lifted weights together, tugged
and pushed the barbells high up, into the paradisal pacific sky

so dense with cataclysmic clouds marauding over the ocean's
    lathering concourse of waves, crashing to shore.

And men, dressed shabbily in drag, abolished themselves to a kind
of farcical ornamentation because they were dressed in littered fabric

and large black refuse bags,

and when I gazed back at them, before leaving the beach, I thought
they resembled a conjuration of dumpsters.
Some assemblage of plasma.

    Along Sunset Avenue,

I watched a boy inhale the meth by himself like a feral pariah dog.
His gray fingers, cupping the glass pipe with a sphere on its end
    where, in the after burn,

some smog escaped just after he pulled
        his slanted mouth away from it,
           burning him—seemingly—
        in the rancid heat.

And when I saw him light it again, the crystal meth liquefied,
and he moved his small yellow lighter
        back and forth in front of it

as he inhaled the vapors until his eyes lids
        dropped shut

like a sickly salamander.

———

Keats, you know, wrote so dizzy, mixing the senses

especially in that poem *Ode On Melancholy*
        where he asserts

"but when the melancholy fit shall fall from heaven
like a weeping cloud that fosters the droop-headed flowers all,"

        I think he might have been seeing this boy addict

crouching down in the shadows along Sunset Avenue, near the fast
Pacific Highway, while delivery trucks thundered past him
        in dust clouds.

    I think
I was unstoppable in my *own* lostness, clothed in my own vapor

when I found myself adrift in the canals, mesmerized
by the brown saltine waters until it hit me I was trapped, too,

by the distinct boutique of the abyss.

And the boy's smoking of meth—
like some initiatory departing of himself into lost vaporization—

turned me obscure and transparent, like I was just blue condensation,
        mist, fog.

Nothing left of me but drowsy salt-light.

And, kneeling beside a white flower in a pot, I felt
        the structure of the world

bending me down, so fraught with all these irreconcilable ideas
        and impregnable deities

without actual names and, while a woman watered her plants
and the silent canals flowed memoryless—without interpretation—

I became *remote,* like the meth addict boy, lost in translation, without prayer.

———

        On the beach,
        far off,

rain collected over the pier and a police car rode silently up to it.

Another woman, a nightingale, talked sporadic into her cell phone

as I walked up to the pier to drown myself in haze.

And the Caretaking Angels—those beings sent to gather
all of us poorly born to flesh again—

crouched in ranks along the shore, readying one by one
to cradle me into their extended gentle arms: I could see them

in the wave's bloom and sprawl.

And the rain fell silent, like the hungry splintered spirits
        of us all.

10. The Angel of Strange Loops / Rumbles Me Awake

The angel of rumble me awake / rumble me awake had told me
I was just a strange loop, just a series of activations that can be

made more active in the future.

Does this mean the brain is just a programmable holograph made more vital
by the working hands of mystery?

By odd gestures of God?

        By the pull and thrust of romantic love?

Does it mean the sunrise, shimmering off of the Atlantic, will still resemble
dandelion and orchid strips of bark

as I peel them off, one strip after another, and lay them over the sand?

Does it mean each kiss I offer to my wife and receive back from her
will loop me into a complete new set of synaptic wirings?

Does it suggest I'm an open-end canvas? A programmable code?

———

Something in me awakens every time I see where my body is alive
and where it isn't yet.

Each snippet of another's kiss—like my wife's—makes me capable of
carrying her a little farther along the way.

We are each other's suitcase, said the angel.

Every depth contains a multitude.
That's Whitman, said the angel as we walked arm-in-arm past a ruined wall

in South Carolina—this was years earlier
        when I was a blind necessity attaching myself to matter

because I couldn't order the strange world to suit what was so incontestable
in me—namely, that I could be utterly inhabited by other actual lives . . .

and the angel slipped its arm in mine; we knelt down
to where the sea flowed like a woman's wet garment into a small eddy
composing and undressing itself in the sand;

and the angel sadly whispered to me, ah, well,
       you shall be struck in the mouth by the heat
       of the labyrinth, by the vast multitudes, by beauty,
       you will be clothed in it / a costumed man /

and you'll be penetrated by its tender armies and by a holographic design
that turns you into other people, even into these adrift sea shells,
       into these small innocent turtles

creeping out of the rolling waves like armored souls
       onto the beach. You will walk into every expanse; become it.

~

And you shall be spun awake by the multitudes.
And you shall be undressed in it / unraveled even / stunned / awakened.

———

Every sunset you experience will maim you where the fixity of the self
falters, wavers, trembles, receives the gold
       in the one offered chalice and then lets it all go—
the angel whispered to me. This will be the situation of your eyes . . .

~

Ah well / the angel murmured /
this is how you shall be created / it said.

And you will rise into a sense of bewilderment until your mind
knows the magnitude / . . . of the beauty / . . . of this world
as it falls like so many teenaged stars all over you,

and you will be rendered obedient to it, to its power,
until you are the speed of light where a body truly is and isn't / yet,

this is just your pilgrim's way . . .

And you will come to know your part in the unraveling of all beauty.

———

And you will be made into the images of the world and its thousands
of hours as they are laid down into you . . .

just as the shore is a tapestry—inescapably—of this itinerant light.

Just as the rays of sunset become walkable strips of beach sand.

       Just as your face . . . increasingly . . . resembles

your wife's face / *her eyes* / looking into you / at dark.

Her eyes, blinking your face into you. There is no separation.

———

A few children had rushed by us as the angel told me all this.

The light surrounding us was anonymous. It was a silence.

It was silver and gold at the same time. It was a permeable empathy.

A subversive mirror without attachment.

Rumble us awake said the angels.

Rumble us awake / awake / awake.

Then you will know the condition running the world / running you.

And then, far out—this was on the Atlantic—

I could see the strange loop of the sea's uncombed waves

rumbling in me / in you / oh yes.

III.
Shape-Shifting:
The Art of Changing the Picture Inside the Frame

"Through the branches of the laurel
I saw two naked doves.
The one was the other
And both were no one."

—Federico Garcia Lorca, "Casida of the Dark Doves"

Twelve Quick Soliloquies on Identity & Truth

1.

"You *are* the squirrel," he whispered to me as we crouched there, fifteen feet up in a tree, "& so, construct the shelter as *he* does, by weaving found materials together."

2.

". . . & you are the melted membrane," the paramedic offered to me as we both held the dying woman who'd been hit by a car "&, so, hold her until she is vapor; &, I promise, something of you will expire, along with her, & some of her will *become* you," he said. *& that's love.*"

3.

In the illness, I couldn't remember where it was I'd lost my keys & that is because a virus is sublime & surreptitious &, as I slipped on the wet tile—
the illness haze invading my life like I was a permeable cell—*I lost a minute; I was* the open cell.

4.

"What *is* identity?" I asked the prisoner of war—just a veteran I'd worked with—& he said, "It's a semiotic flow; it assembles & reassembles in a dark cell. & the afternoon birds, chirping, seize it. One learns it Inhabits the Other &, it must needs be. Other is the *other* design—the mystery—by which we see the reality as it is."

5.

"Other?" I asked. "Yes, 'Other,'" he said. "Other is what argues against the literal. Other is a domain of seeing," he said, "because we try to *forget* or *omit* what construes us," he added, while marking the table with his fingers. "Other un-solidifies a fixed dream. Other opens the perceptual."

"And Identity is a just fixed dream attempting to consolidate that which isn't actually real, or even shapeable, except inside this illusion of the Self, which, I'll tell you," he gnarled at me, "has no immediate future except this particular road we're on toward death; toward demise. You see, Other—real Other—is uninterrupted light. Identity = the wrong premise. We're empty."

How to survive the intolerable hours? I asked him, & he leaned toward me, cigarette in hand, & he confessed, "we can act as a distance & return & enter the hours & grant all power to a co-convergent speed & slowness . . . & that is the patience of survival . . . to stop literal time. Expand into all such space."

6.

"Identity is rupture; & it is so porous," my wife admitted to me after the orgasm. "& all the images of the world aren't anything like language. They are amoebic. I am a shape & a shapelessness in spatial-spiritual play, . . . I am Being / being musical."

"Do you remember our wedding?" She asked me one day . . . "& how—just as the bagpipes started up—even though we came ready-made to be wed, *we permeated?*" Yes, I said. We kept our individual selves out of a habit, but now we identify as only *permutable*. In-between snapped finger & thumb. Yes.

7.

Does that mean *all* identity is a fluid? I asked the prisoner of war. "No," he said. "It's *more:* we're Momentary. & we Traverse; &, in the prison cell, we try to grasp it, to no avail, because Time is a small centipede in the corner. It takes the *I* away from itself, & it runs with it. It's hide & seek." Laughter.

8.

"To build the shelter like a squirrel you must *thicken the frame,*" the survival instructor instructed. "Weave *each thicket.*" Ok, I said. & so all afternoon I strengthened each thicket in the shelter so no wind could invade it. Even the law of "just as it is combination"—*which is hawk vs squirrel*—was settled . . . "& I want you to know this," he said: "The building of the shelter is like an *image* of the squirrel's den. It's by an *imitative* means. & it is an imago of *one* type of shelter—but it doesn't allow for human error, i.e., the slip & fall . . . of, say, *gravity*—which is physical truth, which is always truthful. & it's Chaos & Order; both / . . .& so, this active characteristic in us to *latch,* or to hang on, or cling to something, is humbled because the pulse of Chaos is also a necessary energy, it is a necessity of unraveling. We build any shelter out of structure & chaos. Every shelter is structure & chaos."

9.

The mime mimicked a transgender individual walking past us both. The mime said: "*He / She / & They /* are always amorphous & that is because we are network: we're just nerve fibers on a filament that grids itself into the Undifferentiated." The mime said this to me in Washington Square Park . . .

"& so a variety of gestures represents us, & that's contrary. & it's always unpredictable," he said. "Mimes *become* shape-shifters," he said to me as he wiggled himself into a long-bodied barn spider . . . "& watch me as I shake so much—hanging here from my assassin's thread—that both me & the web blur . . . watch how we vanish into thin air. Poof."

He was homosexual, by his own admission. & he said: "Violence against me mimes me into an adaptability . . . & it is a kind of periphery arrangement that I'm modeling for you—& it is the way the self / identifying / dis-identifies with form & / vacates & re-shapes it . . . survival efficiency is periphery arrangement."

10.

One night, on a crisis line, I spoke to a kid who'd jumped from a bridge so *he / she* could meet *his / her* father . . . & all he/she could say to me—by way of an explanation—was that the pronoun-identity released itself . . . & "Whatever I am / or *was /* or became /. . . felt like image music," he / she / I & not I / said . . . & *I* asked: So the Self / Truth / & Identity . . . all these are musical? . . . & the I & the not I / said: "Well, what is learned is that the Self tries to reproduce—by habit—all the mapping of an order that can secure it.

. . . a truth, btw, that the I & the not I . . . . now fully believe is quite *deceitful*. It's all a BS map." . . . & *that* map wants to be drawn fixed & writ secure on a cell-wall—which is what identity believes itself to be . . . but because the wall is musical, & because it is part of the Gloria in Excelsis . . . it shape-shifts us . . . up / & down / & sideways / . . . & it throws us into hap-hazard choral arrangement . . . &, you know, how can a self be solid when it's so thrown? when it's just tossed music? . . . tossed music that mimes a body, a faux gender, a conceptuality, a name . . .

& the truth of that is *Physical* . . . / & all this faux-identity—this role playing, playing itself out in the psycho-sexual / psycho-social-identity politics of our Selfhood—is & is *not* . . . Which is—mind you—neither good nor bad; no, it just is . . .& a body learns that this faux identity is part of a big stage play. The body learns that it holds a hexed bewitched, attractive spirituality *too*. & that is *much more* interesting than all this pronoun clinging we do . . ."

11.

Does the body, at death, halo into a libertine vapor? I asked the paramedic as we lifted the dead woman up onto a stretcher while the AM traffic started up again at the red-going-to-green traffic light—as if nothing horrid had even happened—& he said, "it's just another day for me &, yes, we switch places w/a future which is float-time accessible—like vital light streaming through a cell wall—which is what the brand new life of *anything* always is; & so, *yes,* she will come to you again: perhaps as your wife, singing in the shower. There is no end to how we reify attractive beauty on each others' faces. But it's also true that some of her dead essence will become the red smile of your wife's wet face. It is true. Yes.

"Clean white sheets for us in the morning," my wife said to me. "& some time later we will intermingle & trade shelters again." & then she said: "two forms derive: & to be wed is to decode / like vapor, / like atoms. & it is just life & death, in the various forms of sexuality and nuptial." & then I said, "personage is a formation of appearances that come & go, like illusive arrows: we're just intersections of concurrence . . . & that's everything, isn't it?" & she said: *Yes*. We mask dance to *"The I /The Other / and The Us."*
& then, Who is there? Who? *Yes. So True.* Who?

12.

"Identify without illusion is a liberty-vapor, it's an unbound rhythm inside an energy design," the prisoner of war confided to me. "& it's never fixed. & that's personal freedom." & I asked him, *why?* & he said, "How the hell do I know—I'm not God." & for the rest of the afternoon he sat silent, serene and smoking and staring into the liberty vapor of a sunny, if overtly calm Arizona afternoon. A motionless cat, snug on his lap.

St. Teresa of the Woods

It was a long time since I'd been alone.
Years, since I'd seen her in dive bars,
in cemeteries, alone at dusk's lofting or
in the wild, astonished gaze of hens,
just before their red necks were cut,
the rest of their bodies, jerking in tongues.
After I disrobed, waded into the river,
the light flared like mescaline in the trees,
it orbited, lifted up, became like a sensation.
My whole body felt enrobed in enormity,
like somehow I'd become an amulet.
I'd wished for the power of fire immunity.
To be harbored in auric light—protected
from my own fire, or from another's fire.
She'd worked herself into another country.
What led me here, to the water, was vanity,
and the same trance that says, blocking fear
is a victory. If I was deluded, or if I was
involved in the angle of light, or in the *angel*
of it, which some refer to as *Satan,* it was
because the sadness in me deemed it so,
and therefore, I was beholden to it, for a while.
And when she presented herself to me—
in that hermitage, in that garden she'd
built and planted for her divinity, over there
on the other bank, which to me resembled
a ceremonial tuft of yellow flowered bellwort
rising from mud and fallen logs, near some
lonesome red columbine too, growing softly
in the androgynous shadows of the forest
and above some cast-off hypodermic needles
where she'd injected herself with the drug
that could lift her up out of her delusion,
and carry her into another face of invisibility—
I saw her first as a congress of shifting light,
and then, as an analgesia, a column, a beam,
bringing to me a solemn calmness, a disguise
that ennobled me in quietude, in silence.

There were small bowls of peaches there,
and portable shrines, and a few holy books
where she'd marked bent pages for herself
to read and to study, and there was also a plate
of bones and feathers, and a lively costume
she'd adorned herself in for a ceremony,
for some abandoned erasing of herself,
some annihilation of her lesser personhood
and her alignment with pure holy vacancy,
and when I asked her what it was for,
she gestured that I cease in such questioning,
for it was nearing midnight; the moon, up.
For a moment, I saw the world's playing fields
in her sallow cheeks, saw in her lips a life
starting over, and that we could bear ideas
until they no longer served any true purpose
and then, we could *undertake* consciousness,
as if dangling in one hand, a writhing snake.
And that her long pale wrists were tattooed
with a script I couldn't read, and that she was—
in her form of *will*—becoming wordless,
a totality of hypnotic, ethereal, undiluted light.
A person no longer concerned with idealities,
but perhaps rather, with the *Logos of Grace*.
She asked me, should I give myself over,
would you refrain from touch? And I answered,
touch is what reveals the other, the you, to me.
It is in the eye of the finger, the skin's heart;
it's the simple way we identify a truth; and she
said, you are un-calm, still, and too eager,
still believing you can claim, from ego, what's
the domain of spirit telling deeper truths,
and she softly floated back, away from me, so that
I could feel the delusion, the antipathy in me
that had *shaped itself in my fingers,* in my pose.
And when I moved closer in, to try to feel her
heat, that asterism of glowing within her, she
waved me off, showed me her distrust of me,

and down, in the river's sunken glow, my own
distrust of myself, which was in my own eyes;
my face looking upward, at me. And she said,
you must enter your nativity, your birth again—
so that you can see your *hell,* your commands,
but also that *other,* that touchless witness.
The stranger, whose hands read your palms.
Who guides you through the *threshold's gate.*
Brings you to reconciliation with yourself.
This is your confessor, your vocation, bear it.

My Horoscope in a Style of Harry Houdini

The horoscope read, "you wound up
in this situation because somebody
else wanted it." So let me tell you how
to *escape* it: you lay the white cloth out
on a table by your bedside. Then you
mix the white powder you have dutifully
purchased from the dealer, in 20-mg
of water, and, then, filter it through a
small balled up piece of cotton. Then,
take the needle and flick all the air in it
to the top and push it out. Then, with
the red headband in hand, tie it over
the top of your left arm so that a blue
vein bulges out enough to pierce it,
and insert the tip of the needle at just 20
degrees, and, then, inject the solution
into your vein there. In a moment you
will feel a wind to which no angel has
seen or felt. And then you will fall out.
Something in your mind will lose rule.
And then your evaporation, your escape
from all this, will be complete. Yes.
I have told you this to stir your notice—
says Houdini, unwrapping himself
from ropes. This is while I am alone
in a room in Detroit, the old heaters
rattling the building with steam.
And this is at a time when I am without
name or number; I am anonymous.
And to be anonymous is the way that
advantage seizes someone; rules them.
I watch Houdini walk straight up a wall.
The woman downstairs, intoxicated,
starts singing the song *La Vie En Rose*.
I believe, in her sorrow, she sings it to me.
Houdini sets a cup of tea for us. Says—
and I have captured you, in this drug
imagery, because to escape yourself
is to unravel time. And those who try it,

try it too often with drugs or gambling,
which is a foolish bid for bad blood.
And so you must push yourself in—
to this beer barrel of your body's jar—
and then tie off where your arms rule
all your certainty, and then you must
insist that someone—*your lover is best*—
push and lock the top of the barrel over
you, and then secure it tight with nails.
You must be fixed inside a circumstance.
It's only through fixity we discover a *spirit*
in us—which must be accessed to escape.
And then—inside the barrel's prison—
you must *see* yourself in a vision where
the entrapped light in there is just a
lonely hobo clinging to you. And then,
when terror strikes you like a match and
you're lit aflame—a tree igniting itself as it
stops disputing all that aggresses against it—
you will inhabit the silence it takes to
achieve your horoscope's benevolent
refrain; this escaping, of another's wish
for you. And after you have fell to quiet,
which cannot come through injection
but rather, must come from a lawlessness
only a self-devotion provides to you,
let your hands rise up to the lid's rim
and push it open, for it was always
just a cloud you thought was wooden,
such is the falsehood of all illusion—
just like this selfhood you are alive in.
Only *after* will you know a true limit.
And when I blinked my eyes open to
find Houdini in there—in this room
where I believe he died in—all I saw
was a wall clock that read five o'clock,
a Monday. And the river was slate gray.
There was no sign of Mr. Houdini. Just
the sea gulls, wailing their usual song.

St. William of the Artists Studio

I see him usually in a corduroy coat and pulled cap,
disheveled, unshaven, unruly, his coat pocket
filled up with a bottle of Kessler's whiskey.
Take notice of him on curbsides, in desolate
structures of town where the shoddy pool halls
collect weather-strewn patrons, sorrow's fools—
women who have loved too much empty promise—
who hold impregnable hopes that mark nothing,
and men whose lives resemble broken tables;
just piles of violent uprisings, tumbled to floor.
They refuse the rule of the *intermezzo* where life
could take them into a sweeter emotional salvation.
It's as if they don't uncover the Universe's true way.
I am shocked when he speaks in such symbolism.
They become a *fundamentality* of their body only—
he says to me, his eyes bleak with beauty and longing—
like great, gross anatomies of angst they do weep.
He tells me he paints these people, like bodies
without souls, or like flowers lost in factory smog.
Tells me he becomes *libertine* to address semblance.
That he's shaved his head for the leaving and he's
reading Jean Genet. His colors resemble Soutine.
That art is the process of detachment from the actual.
I see him at his easel, in a studio, oil painting
that ballerina again beneath a lime green archway;
she's his divinity symbol, his statuette of time's
ineffable sovereignty; and I watch him erase her,
start over again with the moss green tutu, her angel
wings rising like triumphant arches from the expanse
of her small body—heavenward—like she's igniting
skyward into a supernatural moss flame of divine rapture.
He leans inward toward me, whispers you cannot
experience art—this representation of semblance
without losing yourself in it; and I answer, I have
not found it, this sovereign symbol like you have—
this special icon of magic where art salvages you;
this small ballerina whom you adore, falter under,
equivocate into a greater and lesser semblance,

and, finally, distribute in a sentience of glowing,
on a stretched canvas. He says to perceive freely
is to court abandon, the disruption of the senses,
which of course is Rimbaud, and at the edge
of the bar where we visit, he draws on a napkin
the figure of the ballerina, and tells me she is stolen first,
and then she is appropriated to image and then,
after she is painted with moss and mauve, is his
molecular woman, the *she* he is trying to become.
I tell him this is Jung, the anima in him and he laughs,
abandons me to his drink of whiskey, and he retorts
to camouflage is not *criminal,* nor is his attraction
to becoming not human settled only in the icon,
the ballerina he is painting over and over again,
but, in fact, is settled in something more mysterious,
the urge to transfigure, like suddenly he himself
is dressed in drag, a figure made of soft rouge
and lipstick, eye liner, and his delicate fingers
raise the cigarette up to his pursed lips. Inhales it.
Blows a series of zeroes into the thin squalid air.
Lays his hand on mine like we'd solve the problems
of the wide world. Tenderness being the heart's
true way. Something in me is transfigured then;
I am attracted to him, want to be with him as a lover,
even though I am as heterosexual as the evening
is long; to which he says is but the way we all pass
between the sexes and the ages inside us—those
corridors of being—and he offers me the lit
cigarette and I inhale it. Love him forever.

St. Chopin of the Vacant Buildings

Alone and walking, my heart full of dejection,
and a woeful, tormented sense of indecision,
I stop, listen, and I hear someone
playing a piano in an old, vacated hotel.
This is when I am entangled in logic.
My consciousness, a liquid going too solid.
I am trying to believe in form over all else.
My face, engraved in matter's bone-hold.
When I step on the small path to the hotel,
I hear the piano, and a voice calls to me.
It says: *you want to hide from an unbound rhythm,
and it's because you are so afraid to be alone—*
he can see me, this man, through the open
window where he is playing a piano—
and to be alone is to face a face of *vacancy.*
You cannot survive without a face
of vacancy is what he is saying to me.
I stand there watching, listening to him.
Deceit is the mother of vanity, he murmurs,
his slender hands the color of rice vinegar
as he gently fingers the piano keys. His left hand,
pressing steadily in a faithful momentum,
his right hand, like an unfaithful bird,
roaming peripatetic across the remainder
of the piano keys. I hear him, before
I enter the broken doorway of this empty
hotel: its floors, ash-strewn, its walls,
stripped of wall paper and paint, and one
chandelier hanging down from the ceiling;
it hovers over the piano he's playing.
All around him are sheets of musical chords.
Some have notes, some have words
in foreign languages. Some are improvisation.
You are a *persona* above an emptiness,
he says to me, and you're lonesome for
one more reason to deceive yourself.
And that is how you will fail in art.
You *falsify* your emptiness by fear; it is not

your fault, he says, but you refuse to risk,
and this is your presumption, your dogma.
You refuse the call to *unmask,* he says.
He gazes beyond me as he asks me
do I believe in the arbitrariness of art.
I answer, I believe in randomness, as well
as form. A swallow, high up in the roof beams,
darts low and flies intimate over us.
The last yellow rays of the afternoon
slant through the black window, roam
the sordid walls, settle into a selfish ring.
He looks ahead into nothing. His fingers
find a rubato. He launches fully into it—
loosening its tempo, hesitating a bit,
as if undressing something with his fingers;
some tempo going into a pulse; now, he plays a dark
brooding down, so he can be *constituted* within it,
and he inserts anticipation and a swelled *frenzy*
before overfeeding the melody with a pathos-
going-into-deep-rain—and, in mid-play,
he asks me if I have ever deceived myself
with art. I tell him art is the salvation
of torment, and its recipe, the fulcrum
of a wise spirit—moving to free itself
from a deluded heart, and he moves into
a polonaise, a waltz, a mazurka, before he
tells me art is a vast *continuum* where the soul
wanders, unfaithful to anything that would
contain it, especially those presumptions
that place too much a premium on habit,
and that it—like chaos—awakens, cheats on itself,
vanishes, and relinquishes itself in a random
veiled light, and it reconstructs, like an ever
involuted strand of hair, before it wanders
free again, in order to repeat,
and I ask him should he stop playing
to identify this idea, to which he tells me,
art is form, created from a single idea

like a life, and the rest of it, is *improvisation*—
you must stand alone to accomplish it,
become lost and found again in its haunted
echo until only the night is your confidant,
and all the rest—*the silence*—swallows you,
which is the way creation works. I tell him
he is correct and he accuses me of deceit,
says I use praise to hide from envy,
and that art places a loyalty on chaos
before it conforms, and he stands up
to menace me. What happens next
cannot be spoken, but afterwards, after
he has abandoned the building again,
and I am left looking over his papers,
I read that he says his work is no longer
warbling birds or cracked china on the floor,
no longer the romance of a sweet rendering—
but instead, is the flow of a finer precision,
a magician, divining the audible from the unknown.

The Angel of the I Is Elsewhere Speaks Straight Dope to Me

And she quizzically asks me, who is your real mother?
Not the woman who birthed you, her open heart

just the cause and effect of one night of love,
and not all the young women who mentored you,

their neat eye lashes, like soft sickles cutting the air
as they blinked, like flowers, like bees, in your face.

Not the whirling river in Kentucky you stood at,
its eddies like galactic flakes, cosmic flux, fire;

and not that deer that walked up on you, once
when you were sleeping beside a dead fire, at dawn;

and when you looked up, startled, it seemed to
ask you, with its soft, chemical eyes, to renounce

everything to the morning's unconscious shape.
In the afternoon of that day you saw shoals, flocks,

and swarms of life move effortlessly across space.
Trees concluded the breezes without a leader.

The I in you is elsewhere, she said to me, that angel
of nonmaterial, holographic memory; and when

I asked where it was, the I in me, she pictured
a sound, gently thrumming across the wild grasses,

and she said, *there,* where the tall tree stood—
projecting, in a shadow, its point of origin far out

past the crumbling fence line of an old orchard—
and when I followed the sound of the shadow,

it fell, soundlessly, underneath a milkweed there,
like children under the age of ten, all sitting still.

And the angel said to me, you are something
other than an organic mass. You are written in

spirit's name; and that other is what you were,
and will be, at another time, in another place.

Go there to find all that otherness that drives you
in your restless fevers; and go to follow the I in you

that both provides to you while it betrays you;
its shape, so ordinary as a face, a body of hunger,

its consciousness unrestricted by material breath,
its mindlessness like a box of suffocating fish.

Go, she said, to the person at the edge of the field,
the looming figure peddling wares there; his suit

made of cheap wool and textiles, his boots the
color of jack pine and bourbon; go to him while

he is speaking in slow-running rhythms and in a high
pitch; and so thin you could poke him right through

with a flute. He is the elsewhere, the I in you,
she said, and he is a mock lecture on a hill that you

will have an endless monologue with; he is you and
he will love you until the mockingbirds above you

frolic in the magnolias, as the ladies walk into town
under their bright silk umbrellas, those covering

their perfect Sunday hair. Frolic with him, for he is
a joke book of fresh details that you'll recall,

later on, while you are with the silent men, minding
your business with them while the groups of ladies

festively nose around the perfume aisles, gossiping.
He is creating a sense of identity, in the bonds of

a true strangeness and a terror that's just the wilderness
in you; and he is just a posed melancholy: a moon bat

that keeps you covered in an I that is not there.
The I is accretive, and full of circumstance; and

that's why it always captures the audience's ear,
she, the angel, said to me. And on solitary farms,

and in the starved emptiness of dead orchards,
the I is in you like a blaspheming bird in a cage.

It loves what it cannot ever own, and it desires
all the irrepressible life self-possession provides to it—

and that is no fault of yours, she said. So enjoy it,
make it a memory of something you can hope for.

Make it something you contemplate when the
voices you hear, after you've left here, start speaking,

and the hundred new faces, waiting there that want
your name, claw and clash and conflict for you,

and one of them steps forward, so perfect, and
it claims a new human body for you to reside in.

Only in that new time will you realize you've
come and gone again hundreds of times, just to

understand that the I in you is emptiness, and
you've come back again to figure all this out.

But today, this day, she said to me, you are here
with me, elsewhere, regardless of what is the same.

Poem w/ the Color of Television Snow Inside It

Who was there, in me, leaning enthusiastically against the Irish girl
beside the 80' Lincoln Continental, the cream-tone color of iridescence—

his arm—mine—scooped around her sloped right shoulder while she leaned
her flat hip—a hip unnecessarily real & made of something that

doesn't answer its name when anyone calls to it—into his rib cage—

& this would have been just after she stood up on a simple tip-toe—19 years
old, & her suspicious eyes aiming to find what parking lot he'd run to—&
she kissed me hello, because she wanted me, wanted me to *want* her,

& the sky, like heroin inside a spoon, blackened. Who was there?

We held white jasmine flowers, sniffed their mist. Caught silk moths.

Who there, in the hard clatter of roaches climbing through palm tree fronds?

The tickle-ripple of the lazy canal, flayed alive by all that incessant rubbing.

Who there, in the twilight blueprint of fish—just lazy gar—shadowing the
surface of the silk canal so that, one by one, the summer stars, so relentless,

bullied the torporific fish until only the maddest stars, like over-turned
crosses of light, rode the backs of the fish down the wrinkled terrain
of the canal until the rural currency of the water discolored itself . . . who?

&, to experience a life—then—meant drinking, caressing one another,
& listening to the radio. & who was there, smoking . . . & staring at us
while we astonished one another, kissed in the fragrant ghost breeze . . .
while the hard headlights of cars electrified the darkness in the park?

~

Once, I saw a man shooting a pistol at the stars, just to use the revolver
as a way to shoot anything blocking him from God. That's what he said.

& sleeplessness is an appointed official, trying to write a poster—
I thought about this once, while handcuffed in a squad car—

& the poster is a gradual patina of who we think we are, defending against diminishment. We abhor diminishment because we mummify in it.

Once, at a motel, I heard a man scraping the green smell of the ocean across the apricot torn walls. He was using a paint scraper. Drunk as light.

He opened the wall into flame. He was pissed off, I can tell you that, because he wanted to be the sea in his *own* voice, not imitation.

& a woman in a manic state—she was a nurse—told me she was gravity, soaring with longing. Her face like a wild horse. Inflating to be the dust.

~

We inflate to be the dust.

Who felt that love sickness that is a jukebox, playing to tranquilized stars? Under the stars, sitting on a box, I remembered the beach as *defiant.*

The tips of the waves resembling snow, crashing into inconsolable falling. The waves defiant: not giving up until, like gray steam from bottle, dawn smothered them into a flat nothing. A flat sheet of defeated angel wings.

Some other voice comes back to me: a man on the beach in a torn gown, hung over. Vacant as a house. Angry at me. At the sun. At the salted hotel.

Melancholy is cheap. He must be starving now. He must be bankrupt.

Who was there beside the boy—new skin inside a new language— as he threw his right arm around the Irish girl, just after she kissed him, her hips flat against him &, in the darkness of the photo, one or two white specks of snow—photo lab errors—floating there. St. Petersburg, Fla.

Impossible. The Continental, big as a mound of white snow? behind us?

Then: I was drunk in a hotel in Forsyth, Georgia. Dialing through the TV. Can I confess that we shrink into the static-fizzled snow-light on a TV?

~

When she cried, the spinning loom of her life seemed impossible. To me.

So I left her crying. There was no surprise in the dark moment. Just me.
It wasn't my life. & I began wondering about God. Nothing begins
in its own voice I heard it say & I didn't want to hear why nothing begins.

~

Then I was a nameless snow falling in Marquette, up north. I waited until it
stopped. & when it was done—everything white—she wasn't crying any
longer, & Del Shannon, *Runaway,* it was there, on the radio. I turned it up.

Everything cuts through the ferry boat's wake in a kind of thirst. I took the
ferry into a small harbor. & I drank with a man who stared across the street
at a woman trying to fit a small coat on her toddler daughter, & he mumbled
to me, *That girl there, you see her coat? She's like Irish sheep. She's snow.*

Beauty lights a smoke. & it forces the sky to jigsaw a coat of crystal-white
stars across the soft water . . . & the living & the dead are the same in a
photograph.

~

Who answered me, later, in the mountains when the wind turned the spines
of trees
into black tar sludge? The crickets chirruping, like red light down a ravine.

Who is the lonely boy that hungers inside a tea spoon? Without history.

So I heard shrieks & screams. & I threw stars all around so I could plunge
headfirst down a weedy gulch & land in a mound of tuneless white snow
& be dissolved & love something at the same time & still not care.
& be invisible inside TV static, snowing myself into something that isn't.

~

*The snow is enchanted in its own story; it is dead & its always cold, & the
little girl is a sheep & so the woman, her mother, must close her eyes & wipe*

*a table clean. & serve coffee & toast to truckers—highway men—on rest
stop breaks. & obviously, the loom is in the lane anyway, & there's nothing*

*you can do about it, it's just the way music, climbing through parking lots,
softens the shot at the same time as the fatigued aftertaste of it all amplifies*

*us to get up from a sprawl; & try again for the reach into the wild light that
soars with a pensioner's longing. & the snow is blossoming cherries anyway,*

*it's faith in a sheep's clothing; & so you can fit yourself into it, just to get a
handful of it & never stop trying it out. & I couldn't explain it to anyone, so I*

*read the paper, drank, & listened to my own breath filling up a dark house
with a bankrupt official waiting inside it, counting out the letters of his name*

*until dark smoothed it, made it soft like a bed worthy of sleeping silently in.
& outside a smallish apartment, church bells will ring & say, it is all wrong.*

What I did or I didn't do. & to become TV static white snow is to be what's already gone. It is an empty chair. & who was it, beside me, smoothing out my name?

~

What I remember isn't what I thought it would be. Not one bit.
I think stiff tears—silence—guards a tuneless snow, falling in a window.
A window in Cheyenne. Or Roanoke. A hotel in Pittsburg. Or Delaware—
where I held a boy as he tried to kill himself with a camping knife.
We were by a river, & he was pasted over with rotted leaves & sweat
& high on too much of a substance I couldn't get him to tell me about,

& all I could think of was going up-town to score some minky.

It's tuneless. The snow. & it has brown or red eyes & a ruined dress
              & it says,
              Walk away Renee.

The song is tuneless, I'll tell you that, & it hides inside the snow. & it's a blueprint for something that's always missing.

& that's what I saw when the Irish one was crying, something was missing.
& I couldn't will myself to find it. It hid in a song. & my eyes didn't dare.

Betrothal

The difference between then and now could be that now I am listening. And I am hearing with the lonely boot camp of my ears the song of a formlessness shaping itself in my body. It isn't me. Or is it? Maybe it is you.

Love, whispered the visitor, is a shapelessness. It is spirit's insignia.

It holds my crooked face in its tulip hands and it blows smoke into me.
All around me. It is maybe at most 19,000 days.
Spirit precedes the body. It gathers us in its gloved hand. Makes us.
We are its fickle toys. It animates us for a while. By love we come alive.

The ships in the restless harbor pulse the whole wide world.

I am smelling the sea drying at shore. I'm remembering what made us:

How the quick, timeless wind lifts a letter I wrote to her before I met her, there, at her back door, her hands shoved deep down into her blue jeans as we first kissed. As the spin and whirlwind created us.

That we paused there to wait for something:
a quiet eternity where our hands—together—(our palms, just boned ovals of self)—made small tinkling sounds across the tight face of water as we crushed and dropped our names into it.

That water-mirror: two names entered it. We held hands so tight to jump.

Is that the water, is that the steam? In dizzy eyes and ears where we stand, dwell, swim, release?

Is it in the steam where the wind-chimes dwell? Do I feel its bidding?

Betrothal makes starburst, is hot steam. Where Spirit spirals home.

To let go purls us into fluid. We wiggle like a ladle wet with jasmine.
Our names burst like blooms of lavender tea, across a spider-web of sky.

Anthony's Moss Piglet Water Bear

We survive, the boy told me, because we can die.
I've been researching it, he said, because my
hamster died & it's quite likely my fault; I let
him go too long without water. I found him dead,
in his cage, & that's why I'm here, to talk to you.
My hamster didn't know how to come alive again.
The world scares me & girls confuse me, like,
should I cut farts around them or act serious around them?
My mother says I feel guilt about my hamster,
but guilt doesn't explain why I feel so confused.
Guilt acts like it knows too much about everything,
especially everything a girl understands just by snickering.
& it is the water bear, the moss piglet, that can
survive anything—intense heat, terrible cold, thirst,
lonely space—that I want to be, he said. & why?
I asked. & he rose, stood alongside me, drew me
a picture, a cartoon of the bear. It resembled, in
fact, an actual little bear, floating in a pearl of water.
Look, he pointed: I can erase it, the water mass
surrounding the bear, the moss piglet, & the piglet
bear will shrivel up into a sleep state—it's almost
like hibernation but my father, who sits real quiet
at night when my mother watches TV, calls it silence,
'meditation,' which is what I think the piglet does,
it meditates, which I think is a kind of waiting,
until the pearl of water encircles again & awakens
him. The piglet can freeze or dry up, it's in a tun state,
which is a kind of a dead state—in between alive
& not alive—that waits. & can you help me do that?
the boy asked. Why? I asked. & he answered, sir,
guilt is not enough to make up for letting my red
hamster die; to make up, I have to go without water,
become a pellet, a durable moss piglet water bear.
Why a moss piglet water bear? I asked him again,
& he didn't say anything at all to me. He just
drew the bear again for me, shriveled up, its eight
bulky arms holding death, desire, all this big life.

The Angel of Let Me Remember My Name

told me that the form of the name is a feather
and in this poem I have to mix a feather
with a love object and a wall. This must be
one of the formulas of love. And so Anita
and I tried to fix ourselves to the edge of a bed
in Natchez—after she posed for me—
she was topless and smiling into the universe—
which was a lovely thing to do and, so bold,
after so many years of being married,
and because America relies on rivers
to allow it to accept change and desire, she
walked me down and over to the cliff
where the old Mississippi River wound
itself around love and heartache and desire,
just to show us the angel of let me remember
my name. Here's the thing: the name is a feather.
What does this mean? Maybe it's that we are
a feathered transience, brief and beautiful,
and moving downward, on a river of time.
Maybe we become naked as we age out.
Maybe we flare one more time with the gift
of youth; we're naked with abject desire.
That's what the river said, but America can't
get a grip on things that aren't solid.
And most men, I fear, can't get that either.
But the Mississippi wound itself around
a love song and, on the lower banks,
we could make out a name, forming itself out
of mud and nonsense; and oh, about that wall,
that's me. I'm the wall. I'm just a construct
of bones pushing against freedom's air.
I fear it takes years to un-roll one's walls.
And when my fingers caress a flower's petals,
my bones freak out and shudder; they can't
accept the wind moving like the breath
of life through a petal or the way it
actually ripples through the river's soft
seductive bounce *in* the purple flower;
it's just that we can't handle the name in us

that's evaporating. And about the feather:
this is what the angel said: she said the feather
is the name, plucked. All feathers tether
and pretend they belong on a body. I've never
met a feather that identified as a bird.
Mostly, any good feather seeks to take flight,
which is exactly what the name tries to do,
especially when one is deeply in love.
Anita said: kiss me like we have no more nights.
Kiss me like we have no names at all.
So I did, and we both became nameless.
And we walked together, nameless, out there.
I found a dead feather on the side street
in Natchez, just beyond the cliff where Anita
and I gazed down at the Mississippi,
which resembled a wiggling brown feather
pulling itself away from the land.
And hoisting the feather up in my hand,
I twirled it in between my fingers
and I was a bird then, but I didn't know it;
I was bird in inter-play with air and flight.
Even my birth name seemed arbitrary.
I had no name. No name at all. Nor her.
And Anita slipped her hand into mine
and suddenly we were in that bedroom
in Natchez, becoming mindless, just
like the Mississippi was / is mindless,
stripping and pulling itself off the land's
body so it can roam free—nameless—a name
undressing itself, just like us—her and I—
alive and free in that bedroom. But if you've
read this far into the poem and you've been
a feather too, a slice of life fixed and then
ripped off of a governing body, you'll
know quite exactly I'm talking about;
you'll know the pleasure of being free
with a mate you're stoned in love with.
You'll know what I'm taking *into* myself
from the angel of let me remember my name.

The Obscure Darkness of Inanimate Things

Now they are gazing high up into twilight to catch the birds there, and he,
just now, softly touches her shoulders—she's in front of him, they're

sitting quietly together on a bench in a little park outside of a favorite church
of theirs, one they visit whenever they're traveling again to this city—and he

pulls her to him, closely, so he can feel her breath heaving soft across his
knuckles as she sighs, as she releases all the tension and the weariness

of the day and she rocks backward, into him, into that old security of his
chest, and, without words now, because they already know it, this familiar

safe intimacy, she cups both his hands in hers so that they're sculpted, joined
as one, and accepted just like one of the stone statues of saints placed here;

and a flourish of coal-black birds ascends up and over and across the pointed
church steeple in a flight of ink so that both of them see the one dark smear,

a transposition of inked lines soaring across, around and beyond the steeple
and past the rounded dome of the church behind it, so that when she turns,

abruptly, to tell him some secret, some confession she's been withholding
from him for maybe a month or a fore night and she kisses him too, melts

herself into him, offers quick soft kisses too, across his moist opened lips,
the newness of it is just too much—it is carnal knowledge again, it's saying

one thing and yet meaning completely another, and it points to everything
else; and it's what they do when they join together and fall into that trance

that unites and unties them, just as the bells of the steeple start ring-banging
loudly, madly, breaking the whole sky open; and the black birds become

the history of two beings rising upward, over that little city park outside the
church and then over the wet stone paths that blend into gardens until they

cross the fresco walls that hold the wild souls of the saints so immortal—so
that what is remembered is faith, or desire, something that can't ever be

forced because they're in the temple of time—the enormous mindless space of it—and all that is happening in the universe is in the body *too,* theirs

right now, so that when they complete the kiss, there is a dream that hides the world from them so that they can, again, grow a seed in the heart of the

earth between them, and it's an exodus back home—something privately kept in bundled hands that hold enough harvest in them to feed them deeply

when they are lost stowaways—through the obscure darkness of all those unexpected, un-foreseeable, unanswerable, inanimate cold things.

IV.
Contemplations:
Chasing Names on Nameless Water

"The unexpected interest made him flush.
Suddenly he seemed to forget the pain,—
Consented,—and held out
One finger from the others."

—Hart Crane, "Episode of Hands"

Poem with Anguish in It

Everything I'm about to say might have happened,

& if it's true
I'd like to tell you the night never forgets
what it gives away.

& if there was a woman, she committed herself
to a mystery,

& if she walked, wrapped by a shawl into trees,
it might have been because of heartache

or a song she was following.
& if I saw her first, exiting a Super 8 motel
where she strolled self-silent & alone,

I might have even figured to myself she *was* alone,
even if she wasn't.

& things can go wrong, & we enter at various points,

& secrets are what we keep when we have no one
to confess to,
& if that is true, she glided past a dive bar
where the patrons were howling & gambling

& there might have been a man in there
familiar to her, maybe her ex-husband, or her father,

or maybe just her next door neighbor—
a fellow she'd smoke with—

& sometimes belief, dear friends, is all we ask
another person to undress from us;

& maybe one-night-stands are just two strangers,
undressing beliefs from each other

so they can feel free enough to care again,

& I never had a one-night stand
that took away my anguish—

even though a few willing partners tried,
& so did I—

but anguish is just a homesickness
without a door to relieve it. So we fall into it,
& it makes us stronger, wiser somehow.

& maybe the morning is for regret,
& the night is how we make it,

but this woman kept walking out of town

until she was a mushroom shape.
& when she entered the trees

I saw her un-cape her shawl & let it drop
like a burden

& she started running—
not away from something but *to* something—

& maybe release
is what all the sadness is truly asking of us

& I couldn't see or hear her

but there was a light, & I think it was over
a river

where a big water tower rose up,
& this is where I'm making the rest up

because all I see is her, climbing the tower

where she sees her brother, way up there,
readying himself to jump
to where the hard concrete waits

for his body to hit it, like a meteor.

I guess this poem is about her younger brother.

& so here's the part I tell her:

when someone leaves us, we follow them
until they tell us *not* to, & he hasn't yet,

he hasn't told her; *don't you dare come for me.*
I think he's still waiting for her, he's looking for her.

& here's the awful truth—she has to say *please don't do it*
to him
because he's going to jump anyway. He's a goner,

& he needs her to witness it—
so he's valued by her, in his last act.

And sometimes people feel so powerless, so alone
that they create a stage-setting for one last act.

& sadness is just a ball of anguish we release
from ourselves in order to know where we begin or end—

especially when someone we love stages a last act—

so that we can enter the human riddle of love again,
& be stronger for it. Somehow, some way, again.

& maybe I'm supposed to trail her,

& shake her a bit & hold her tight,
because he tells me to—
so she has someone there beside her
when he hurls himself into hard concrete.
Someone to tell someone else—like you—
about this ordeal she's gone through.
About her shock.

About all the anguish inside it. & the value for life.
& maybe that's what this poem's about.

Contemplation on Middle Age

I suppose I could find it, what I've lost, if I gaze into
the spotted jewel weed where the summer bees,

floating under the dark-spotted cathedral-shaped orange
flowers dangling from slender stalks, shimmer,

and dragon flies bewitch me, and the wider colony rim
of the farm pond is a painter's palate of wild, beguiling

weed-flowers in kaleidoscopic splendor and, yes, a fishing boat,
floating aimlessly out there, is empty, of course.

Something on the water's mirrored black surface beckons,
but it's just me searching for names on nameless water.

And I suppose I could find what it is I've lost maybe
on a Tuesday, and maybe I might find it in the prairie smoke,

or in a fat-fire burning bin, squealing out an ashy, secreted
wail from the wrinkled metal pit, out there, where the barn

rises red and sturdy in the dusk, and the dolorous cows
moan for me as I pull the buckets of water up—chin

high at my shoulders just on a whim—so they can stretch
their meat tongues into the cold faucet water, to drink—

their loud slurping sounds almost comatose, lethargic,
as I roll from foot to foot, to hoist-haul the bucket up,

my farm boots saturated with Iowa mud, my belt,
pulled tight to hold my jeans around my hungry waist,

my young body not quite as it is now. And maybe
I can find what it is I've lost in the silences, out there

in the rows of corn that anthologize themselves
in coarse collisions of pale green thickness, or maybe

I'll find myself in the after-wind of breezes cutting
through the cornfields' literature of insects, or maybe

I'll find what it is I've lost when I find—again—that
small quaint book I wrote all my voices in, especially

those voices blowing unconsciously through me just
now, their dream-like phrases and sentences chirping

and murmuring like swallows across the fields of corn,
and all the contemplation in all of that, that remains.

Contemplation on Dissonance

Sometimes, at four am, as the stars so sacramental, shine on, I leave my bed, I gather to me a small incremental blanket, & I roll myself in it, in a sad heap in the park, & I stare up at the checker board of night sky as the restless clouds blur & bandage whole open spaces of the universe until the slag-heat of one star, palpating, burns another opening into the galaxy & I see it—the one star—& I try not to believe in it too much for fear of losing it, later on, as the drunken, unconcerned sky bleaches itself over again & the forlorn transport trucks, so loud, down-shift & thunder-roll across roads made for the restless, who race against time, like they think they will actually escape.

& once—alone there & whispering to myself in the soft, confessional prayers of one who is baffled & alone, heart-sick within himself—I felt all the immanence inside me, leave me, & I was, for the moment, in dissonance, like a fog-mood, & I was emptied out of words, like a pint of drained vodka.

———

&, in the third act of one's life, when all the years slur on & we lose sight of the ballet we've lived & danced in, we start to look real good & real hard at who will hold us when we grieve a loss, or we cry, or rage, or fall alone in a room or try to deny that the symposium is almost over, or maybe just beginning to ridicule the curtain.

& that's just the climate of death we feel, a cold chill rounding us at our ankles. Swirling up our bodies like some earth snake from the ground below.

———

Dissonance, she said to me, is like a brief hibernating. We hide—especially when all the feelings overwhelm us. &, in the bathroom mirror, in the private treachery, we see whole birds abandoning our face, whole stars suddenly bleached white by sudden clouds, whole pastorals darkening. & the memoir, the nostalgic reflection, lampoons us. & we hide: we shrink away from it all.

———

Don't be afraid of the dissonance, said the stars. & don't ever hide. Don't.

———

& don't be afraid to take a surreptitious sip—just a quick one mind you—of the sweet whiskey, tucked there in a suit coat pocket, the poet Stephen Dunn whispered to me at a poetry reading—this is all true—&, when I touched his long-suffering right shoulder, he confided in me, "I'm really quite glad you're near, I really am," which I didn't fully comprehend nor understand, other than that he was old, whimsical & a little bit tired by the hoopla, & somewhat dissonant as the society ladies in fur coats bullied up to him, one-by-one, so he could sign his Selected Poems. & he blinked a goodbye wink at me. & he was swept away in a pride of fur coats as the ladies captured him. Made him one of their own.

———

& don't be afraid to enter the fog at this point in your life, I said to me, tucking my neck into a coat collar. The dissonant hooded figure you see in the fog brings to you your final naming, where the flourish of an ending—yours—visits you. Sets the table with a peacock hen. A string of balloons. It celebrates every moment you sipped a whiskey against a night that forgets you; or worse yet, a morning that only recalls what its immediate mouth can name. & the rest of you is as forgotten as a swirl of traffic rounding a corner.

The Future mouths the names the dissonance will find in you, she said to me. Look at it, this hooded figure you see in the mirror in the hallway, looking itself straight into you. Look at it every day so it will give you a glimpse of your new name. & some of the names you'll receive are truly epic, they're quite conceivable; they're what you really you are: for instance:

"Pilgrim Kissed Awake in the Night by Lonely Itinerant Gypsies;" or maybe:

"Angel Unfolding its Wings as Pearled Dragonfly Across Moonlit Water"

or perhaps this one:

"I am the Bewildered Uplift of Vapor, Arresting Freedom from Fire"

or how about this final one:

"Wisdom Mirror: Luminous, Clear, Bright . . . Completely Empty . . ."
Names that search, in the end, for the author's true intention, it says.

&

don't be afraid to let the silent dissonance over-take you; it's fine: night or day always carries a fatal murmur that stops mid-word. Your mouth a soft *o*.

&

it lights three candles on a cup cake for you, sets your still heart to flame.

J, an Elegy in 20 Lines

                                                                           &

when she stretched her skinny hand through the air
              to meet mine,

I saw the real murderer, the head hunter hunting her
              & a pile of skulls
that represented her, afterwards, after the drugs

                                      &

the suicide with mistaken identity, which was her anorexia
              telling her she was an angel bride to hunger,
yes to hunger, she said . . & so, I write to you, to recall you

              to the misshapen afternoon
where we watched the eclipse &, later, sat along

the cement wall of the building so you could tell me
we kill an enemy, anyway & anyhow; & some of us

venerate our victims she said to me, didn't she? So *do it,*

venerate me, she said, smoking, smoking, smoking,

love angel of the strychnine kind, the formaldehyde

              in your body now.
I miss you, though, & the hunger that was your soul,
              blurring into me.

Some Cows & Angels Talking to Me

We were talking and she was telling me of the cows
that her sister and her husband would talk to, back,
when they were trying to conceive that baby they lost,
as if the cows, like something supernatural, were
somehow sacred, or *of* divinity, like some special
four-legged totem. And she was telling me that
when they were bored they'd get up early and go driving—
especially after they'd made their morning love,
and they'd brewed coffee and fed the two dogs.

And they'd feel the land rising and falling under their tires,
out along I-94 where the farmlands were gray dew,
and the morning's foggy mist, flooding the spindly trees,
made the trees resemble ruined cathedrals, something out
of Monet in France. They'd see sharp pointed spires
reaching out toward the light, and she, who was telling
all of this to me, said that her sister would think she saw
strange angels out there, rejoicing with the cows;
and they stood like tableaus, out there in the mist.

And it's because she was *pregnant,* she was awake to new life.

And she was also afraid, and elated at the same time—
bringing new life into the world will do this—because the soul vine,
reaching between here and oblivion, carries within it all manner
of outcome; all types of becoming and unbecoming . . .

Sadness *is* a form of eternity, she said.

Well, if you must, it *is* the form life takes when it's time to
end something from its habitual grip on becoming,
that is, from its insistence on staying in a form—

and I can't remember if it was her or me saying the rest of this—
can't recall how the conversation shifted to the *world*—

and you know this last century *is* a sadness into chaos,
it *is* the form God's taking to *end* something—
all the wars destroying the cities;
all the world's unrelenting famine; its disorder;
all this savagery that ignites into violent passion;

and the fact that the dust bowl out west
is forever haunted—
it's full of graveyard ghosts,
is what John Steinbeck said in that book—
and the water-cut gullies of our bodies,
dusting themselves down to dry little nothings.

"It's all so very *terrible . . . this deadly violence . . .*"

Her or me now shifting in a chair, her lighting a cigarette—
collapsing a dry hand through hair.
The small ticking of the clock, distractible really—
because conversation is invasive to time's quiet drum.

And you *see it* in the paintings of bathers at the rivers . . .
All this emphasis on the contrast of bulk and ether,
and also in the repetition of soup cans lined on a shelf.

Marilyn Monroe's face—everything, *all of it,* so sad.

The transience of existence so dazzling: the lights of Paris prostitutes;
sadness in the bathers at the river, in the echoed silhouette
of the cathedral at Rouen,
and how the church itself *evaporates*—is actually swallowed
by the mist, because Monet saw it that way, it *really was that way*.

He was only telling it the way he saw it—the way it actually was,
because nothing, absolutely nothing created by us
is guaranteed *de facto* life; we're all pre-ordained to vanish—
all will vanish, and be absorbed again into the foggy meadow
with the sad angels and the groups of moaning cows.

For she was telling me this,
was saying that when they'd *lost* the child—
their one and only child—
when it ceased in her womb
and was cast away like a lone pebble dropping all the way down
the long funnel where birth and oblivion
co-exist as the twins of existence,
there's just no turning back—
the young couple explained it to themselves
that it really was the cows, so mournful and dense
and grazing out along Interstate 94, that had *decided it—*
had decided that they'd lose the child.

And now her brow furrows, she's blinked something back,
I've no idea what, for she's corrected herself—
it was the cows with the angels that'd decided it.
Something in them that we must *bear* what we live.
This is what the young couple told themselves.
They concluded it as they drove back home together
from the hospital. Sipped their cold coffee at a kitchen table.
It was the only meaning they could *give,* to losing their child.

For everything in a pair carries this kind of well, *sadness,* she said,
this grieving, this joy and sorrow—
or: this image of the Rouen Cathedral we see vanishing
in the mist before it's gone.

And for a moment—it was fast—I could see it,
I could see that little apartment we were in, my young lover and I,
all those years ago in the summertime heat.
And she was telling me that she'd become pregnant, it was mine—
the dumb little thrombosis of flesh, the miraculous spark,
the orange little light in her, *glowing* . . .
shimmering there like a slice of bright citrus . . .

And how it was we lost it—
gave it back to wherever time truly is
when the living beings, the ones we make, choose oblivion,
and return like an otter's flayed body to the fire
on the other side—
that fertile pyre of reckoning within—
that is, when the space inside us, all that we might bear,
is not quite ready yet, for all the rest.

An Elegy for Robert Wachler

We are talking again on Zoom, his big face
in the rectangular screen, the San Diego sunlight
streaming through the hospital window.
I ask him what it feels like to be dying.
Small dry bed creek of a grin, spreading
at the right side of his mouth, quick glint
of light in his eye. He says, "Oh it feels like wind
invading a suit coat. Just wind, spreading."
"I'm not afraid to die," he reassures me
before I have even asked him the hard question.
"You see, I've been invited into a bigger mystery. I see
where the wind goes, on the wings of a hawk."
"I'll open the gate for you," he offers, quick
sly grin at his mouth, silent smile in his eyes.
Some emotion made of delight, of mischievous mystery.
"But no Shiva face at my Memorial," he commands.
"No morose suffering, none of that nonsense!"
And he laughs, then tears up at the same time,
his right hand, like a towel, rubbing his face down;
smiled sunlight, infused with rain on an afternoon.
And I, too, swell into an Irish sadness, some foundation
of bog and hot wet fire, muddy leaves, tiny dew stars.
And we weep into a naked laughter, a softened rain.
Some sorrow that doesn't even know its nexus,
but only its final, unadorned source, its first luminous sense.
And he says, to me, "Thank you for being with me.
Thank you for holding the unknowable with me."
And he says to me, "fare thee well . . ." blows me a kiss.
The anguish in me, like a star flower lit to flame.
Something of his body vaporing out, some part,
becoming eternal already, just by saying farewell.
How, in this incessant dying, a star is faked by its
very light source and it orbs, it flickers out, thinking
itself dead and gone into the dark, and then comes
awake again—inside memory, inside time, inside us—
inside a name that vanishes, but never ends.
I keep dreaming of almond orchards, of lovers
under falling petals looking all over for the source

of what brings us to life inside a body.
I keep dreaming dreams where owls and hawks
sit in the dark shaded woods, looking for me.
I keep dreaming love is an almond orchard.
And inside the petals, everything in us awakens.
Some months later, after Rob has died,
I sit very still beside him as he rests in his coffin.
It is after midnight, and I am reading him poems.
Death into rebirth poems, traveling poems.
Poems that tell us there is no home in the end,
but only a phantom body that we travel lightly in.
I sit still, paging through all of the poems.
A small group of 72-hour visitation angels—just
twinkling chimeras of snow-crystal and salt—
rest there, all around us: when I look deeper,
I see that the angels are just tiny, barely discernable
shimmering lights in the potted plants, they're
just the indomitable stars, just bonfires, just hues
of a dream we think we live until it leaves us,
and one of the angels comes whispering to me
that, when Judy reached the hawk feather
just behind Rob's head, it completely
opened up his ability to be cared for—
I remember you whispering this to me, Rob,
your voice in a hushed, graveled whisper—
and you said to me, on the Zoom, "Ken,
I've never loved her more . . ." Oh, and the
poems I read to you that night, Rob, alongside
the flesh that burns out while little stars shine,
were poems meant to help you travel, to
take with you every blanket of light worth remembering:
WS Merwin's, "The Anniversary of My Death,"
"A Walk Blossoming," by Jack Gilbert—
who believed we are a small light that gets
larger every moment we stroll closer with death—
and, of course, the great Spanish Poets:
Juan Ramon Jimenez, "I Am Not I," and also
Jose Gorostiza who speaks of an incessant

kind of death—the whole personification
of it, this death rising utterly ceaseless in the
nameless, indomitable stars, "oh intelligence,
oh flaming solitude," he writes, "oh emotion
of aching substance barely hurrying or slowing—"
come move with me as we sail the glowing dark,
and I read to you another Jack Gilbert, that Pittsburg
poet and half-Buddhist, his "A Brief for the
Defense," where he says, no, in fact, he claims:
"we must risk delight—in the face of all
this damn sorrow," which of course, you did.
And I read you one of mine, a long 8-page poem
about how love is just a multiple convergence
of light sources, that we *make* the phantom body—
our enlightened light—through how we conduct
a light most glad of all, and that light takes us up
over the farthest ridge—where a nameless fire
dwells in a shower of stars waiting for us, all along,
and, in love, we resemble a red hawk, seeking the light.
Rob, I keep hearing love in the cathedral bells
and in the hard drumming over stones I can't see
with my eyes. I keep smelling crushed roses turning
into velvet in the apartments where people paralyze
time inside an evening's delight. I keep thinking
love is just a call-and-response motion. An energy design
for its own perpetuation of movement.
On any dance floor in any city, all it says is just this:
"Love names a name in the heart of another"—
and this is the riddle I am thinking that any death solves.
That we are a name we give to another to remember.
A name that nourishes us until it's time to go home.
A man's face on a Zoom call, is a name in me now.
It's a name that fills up the suit coat I wear, like air.
Rob, I keep thinking that love, in the end, is infinite.
It's just a fire that borrows a face and a name for a spell.
A fire-name that spends a short time bowing, celebratory,
to those very special people it loves. A fanfare light.
A fare-thee-well light that rests like a tiny angel

in a plant while I am reading a poem to a man whose
name I loved. A man whose name is opening inward,
toward its own source. A man whose name now
is just another astonished mirror for what spirit
does when it hits unsustainable crescendo, then
fires up up up, into the cathedral of night.
The stars above, like zippers, swallowing it whole.
Rob: I keep hearing a rustle of strange birds
in the shrubs, I keep seeing a wind so intense
it is consciousness. I keep smelling the water
lifting out of the river bed. But that's just me,
standing here in the almond groves, looking again
for that mystery dream in every name I ever loved
then lost again to the white feathers that fan
into silence. That's just me looking for the special
name that vanishes, but doesn't really leave,
because it's already fanned home. It's in me,
and in every other guest here to celebrate you.
It's in us all, Robert, you with the beard and the fine
suit coat. It impassions us, Mr. Wachler, standing
debonair with a cane. And this is just me,
thinking I'll find the dream that is the bearded face
of a man I once talked to on a Zoom call
in San Diego, who then blew me a kiss, and bid me
"fare-thee-well," and whom I now worry I can't find
when, in fact, it will always find me—this precious name—
because it belonged to a man whom I once loved.
And inside a light most glad of all, oh, it will
climb through the torn white sails every now
and then, it will bless me, this name that is the
name that keeps on saying it. This name that
relinquishes all its life. This name that,
in all its dying, offers its light back into me.

We Are All God's Poems #1

& the surety we seek when we long for something lost
inside the providential, radiant chamber of what is holy,
is quite inexact. & it's inexplicable. & it's a disciple to the inscrutable,
& so it's charged & beneficent & wholly without guile,
she said to me, alongside an old, unused set of train tracks
where the fragrant orange groves swelled alive with bees
& the noises there, carnivalesque, festive, amounted to
a bewitched summer song. &, you know, she was a military
widow, just thirty, & her husband, overseas, had been
blown up & killed when his right foot grazed a half-buried
land mine still pocketed there, like an angry, kinked little apex god.
& she'd wiggle her delicate neck locket in her hand & open it up,
& she'd display it to me—his brave picture in there—before it
became a twisted memory, just a diffuse light she could feel
more than ever see in the dark, after midnight, while
stirring her tea with two shots of whiskey mixed in it. & we
were brief lovers. & we were chaperones for one another
as we fell deeper into the scourged unknown &, you know,
hope is an infused aura, she whispered to me . . . & it's exhaled
in the effluvial mass of all the alive dead—those souls
officiating their theatrical memories to us. & we are
all god's poems, she admitted, & then, confessed, while
showing me where it was she'd cut her left wrist in the dark
aftermath of his malignant leaving; &, you know, when I feel
the scar there, where I cut myself so I can feel it & allow his
hot light in, all I feel is a strange, secured bio-luminescence—
just spectra of his Eros in me. & the whole country, at war,
& all the other wounded lovers holding onto one another at dark,
is a macrabiosis of anabolic life . . . & it's so lively, if we allow
ourselves to feel it . . . & we become all of god's poems
articulating who it is we'll celebrate when we let a slice
of somebody's deep-lived library of heart-noise inside us.
We are the one voice of 100 billion voices talking in us.
& maybe that is the contagion of love: we're osmotic.
We are all cells in the body politic of all lives lived in in us.
& we live it: their spark of life in us to its fullest, oh yes.

The Recording Angel & The Angel of History
   (an email fragment)

. . . and what of that Mizocz Ghetto & all those murdered women there, stretched dead like greater *snowdrops flowers* in the cold ravine; it's so malignant, this evil, conducted under the auspices of war . . . Yes, the Angel of History returned; it's catastrophe they're after—because of the ego's fascination, it's preoccupation with shock & awe . . . & oh yes, that recent murder of a Black man, George Floyd, in Minnesota . . . 9 minutes & 29 seconds with a knee to the neck . . . amazing how killing is organized as suppressive recipe . . . it's the spirit force they're after . . . that, & a banal personality cult of law & politics . . . Yes, the Angel of History said . . . & the Recording Angel wrote back: it's a pernicious covetousness that appeals to them, when they are in their darkness . . . and isn't it just the *Apparatus,* that bureaucracy so very evident to those whose oppressed lives live underneath it? the Recording Angel wrote to the Angel of History, and in those countless wars—militarized, politicized, legalized, economized—waged by those who will be chief beneficiary—the elite—isn't it just the faux appeasement of a race, a class, undaunted by its will to power? And isn't it indeed—in the end—just the slipknot notes of a peace without moral purpose or human interest? Wrote the Angel of History back; And The Recording Angel went on: The Imperial interest always wins; yes . . . and then they try to re-write you in their graven image; yes? And, oh do I remember my endless wandering—like a torn nationless flag—through the rubble of Cologne, Frankfurt, Essen, Hamburg, Dresden; and what I saw there—amidst the collapsed, blown down buildings and the mish-mash of torn bricks and bloodied bones—was that what was made was just a convenient "peace of gold, shining inside oil." That's Archibald MacLeish, the poet, correct? The Angel of History wrote back, *yes.* Those bombs created a heat vacuum that burned the history out of whole roads, out of whole bodies; and bodies are the currency of human wars & human suppression, wrote the Angel of History; all wars utilize the body as currency; what they aim to pervert is the spark of Spirit; and what is aimed for is a stealth of precision—a precision emulating a poisonous dot on the raging arrow of greed. And the Recording Angel reported further that . . . what they aim for is the appropriation of the holy chimera, which is only the Spirit's to create; but they cannot help themselves; it's as if the burning of bodies, i.e., the saturation bombing of others by uranium, by plutonium, by napalm, by false vainglorious patriotism slogans and by that sin that has no name but for here and now I will name it as the *grandiose deed,* is the means by which they can *produce* the chimera imago—the sight of a holy body; but it is a body made and usurped by atrocity; a hell seedling; It's as if they're conjuring up a malevolent death . . . by acts of unrepentant evil; It is as if they fail to understand the *nature* of their own causes & effects. And they utilize Politics & Religion to make a *faux rationalized intelligence* of what is, in the end, an unintelligible mystery. *The movement of Spirit.* Oh, and Hiroshima, Nagasaki, Hanoi, Sarajevo, Baghdad, Damascus, Belfast, Gaza: these were cities *infernalized*—is that a word? the Recording Angel asked; and *yes*, wrote the Angel of History: destructive chaos is what is ordained— by and through that which they consecrate in the name and aim of a religio-political faux heroism; it masquerades as valor; and just that, alone, marks them as makers of atrocity; and Klee's Angel Novus, have you seen it? The Recording Angel asked; Yes, that absurd floating angel with the scrolls for hair, wrote the Angel of History back; Yes: it *is* Me. I am history, floating abjectly against a timespell that forgets itself as it is lived and unwound like a string that never ends; I am a function of space and time that cannot contend with itself except by-and-through the pre-given devotion and brush strokes of a consciousness that yearns to be transcended in it . . . [pause] & . . . the winds of change push me into the zone of memory and forgetting; but what of hope? What say, of Anne Frank? the Recording Angel wrote back; [pause] . . . yes, regarding hope, wrote the Angel of History back; I was there; I lay my body down in the Prinsengratch canal; I *was* its face for a while / I stretched my arms out to her as she was a trade wind entering my body; but hope; *yes:* Time destroys the temporal; and loving acts re-write pained memory; . . . do they know this? . . . [pause] . . . memory is the coin I drop into the fountain of eternity; . . . it pays the deed and toll for all the forgotten actions; [pause] . . . the sin they make of time is that they tell themselves they we will live forever; & that something of their improperly understood willfulness—some egoism in them—will never *die* . . . / they are a brutish lot that believe only what a rub of impulse tells them; would that they would listen to us / . . . it is a spiritual forbearance that wills a lemon light—/ that sweet divinity of the soul in its vertical and horizontal urging— / that directs them in our direction; but it can take so many insufferable years of being entranced / and enchanted / and overcome by Illusion to ultimately compel them from there, to here, to *us* . . . yes: The Recording Angel answered . . . *It is late and the almond trees here are blooming but I must tell you one more thing,* The Recording Angel wrote . . . [pause] . . . something of it was made like a sad mustard seed in St. John's wood in 1965 when a boy wrote out a simple love song for humanity—alongside his bed as he strummed its etheric body to life on his guitar; and he called it—that famous song he wrote for them—*Yesterday* . . . Yes, it is that recurring preoccupation that they hold with *reminiscence* . . . / wrote the Angel of History; this *nostalgia* that stirs them into and out of the sleeping dream they live of themselves . . . / What did Wallace Stephens say to his readers in that poem, *Esthetique Du Mal* . . . What did he say? / Oh yes, answered the Recording Angel . . . / I wrote it for you . . . on one of the scrolls of your hair, the Recording Angel answered back; [pause] . . . Stephens said: "It was the last nostalgia; that he should understand . . ." / Yes. True, said the Angel of History. They must understand how nostalgia (homesickness) seduces them; how it tumbles them backwards into false sentiment, so that all their ideas of time end up being nothing more than nostalgic allure in a reflecting mirror, which is illusion . . . By the way, what did Deleuze say? The Angel of History asked? And the Recording Angel: He said, *Lose your face: become capable of loving without remembering, without phantasm and without interpretation.* And in that same vein Deleuze wrote this: "History is made only by those who *oppose* history" . . . Yes, Yes, *true,* the Angel of History wrote . . . and this is always the problem with Greed, with Gain; . . . and it is also true that . . . with . . . the politicization & the revision about the *outcomes* of History that we see the deceit-making in the causes & effects of *all* their outcomes. It is as if they don't know *me* . . . it is as if the Victors put a shade upon the truth; upon the actual . . . but the past, you know, the Angel of History wrote, is a conjurer's talisman . . . / its face is writ on mine and it is made of purity; it has within every crease of it the *actual;* and that's why it is pure . . . [long pause] . . . and despite themselves; despite their attempts to climax their implosive arousal with bombings & distractions & their 1.6.21 insurrections and lawsuits and fake news that re-write it—the past—as if it were a stage play bent like a nylon scroll that could be re-narrated and rolled up & down like a child's simplified eroticized dream & be penciled over with the slogans of the victors . . . [pause] . . . and alchemized by that lot of those who wish to create the chimera body because they don't even know they are lonesome for what's already been degraded into the full measure of their secrecy from themselves; despite all this, they will be called by affliction to awaken and to see; . . . [pause] . . . It is written here already . . . The Angel of History wrote . . . and like a nylon scroll that they could simply open and close because they were uncomfortable with it . . .—as if it were a child's eroticized dream—unfortunately, they must awaken in the shuddering of it . . . and they will be forced inside the nightmare that always follows reprobation; . . . [pause] . . . I don't mean them any harm, the Angel of History wrote . . . It is an enraged dream that guides them in and through their stupors . . . & it is a namelessness on nameless water that they seem to be entranced by . . . & they seem to chase it; & even make it true in their science-fiction dreams . . . even those willing or able to see . . . & It is a love supreme that they are born of; a light most glad of all that gifts & ignites them with the *cosmic-continua* of all these musical cries of egoism & appearance that, in the end, become liberated, no matter what . . . & in spite of themselves & despite all their ills & sorrows . . . [long pause] . . . It's just this . . . this one thing . . . this immeasurable light . . . is what they've come here to finally become lost in, to fumble through, to understand, & to see . . .

We Are All God's Poems #2

                                                    &

if the body was burnt up—if it was the true spiritual body
& it was burnt up in a crime of passion so that it became

a fire, just an orb floating high up over a car set to fire at the
river's edge, in the warehouse district, the feral dogs there

running at the fire at first & then shuddering in the heat of it,
ducking backwards away from it to bark—& if the prosecuting

attorney, the DA, called it a crime of passion, would the
spiritual body, a pink & white *dendrobium transperens orchid*

rising sudden, like an unabashed, unforgettable *ghost-light*
over the steel girders of the transport bridge there, ignite

in flame? so that the innocent people gathered across the river
to watch the fireworks might see it, this divination flame, igniting

like a star? Love seeded the ancestral soul like a mica fleck
in the dirty oil water & it floated there, on top of the water

like a seal of grease. & violence killed all of its kind, so that
what came after, for those not yet to be seen, was spectral,

an ambition of ghosts, a flight whose whole aim was to try,
just try one more time for love before the morning burst like

a baptism of light over the wretched buildings & the muddy
cranes, where bums sought kindness, & not cruelty, among men.

& God sent his only son to this earth to light a fire for a new
Astronomy, which isn't at all what the DA said about the

crime. & we are all God's poems said the one witness, who
saw the car lit to flame & the lovers in it, together, claiming

love to be the murderer & violence to be the witness to it—
& the soul that we call our own is not ill, he said. It is God.

Interview

It was after midnight, in a campsite, & I was alone.
What does God, or Spirit, require of you? I was

asked this by a person standing in the pine clearing.
He didn't offer a name to me. The pot where I'd

cooked hot vegetables in, full now, with stars.
My tent, behind me. & I stood at the edge, looking

at him. *God—which is Spirit—requires offerings.*
Like what? He asked. The ears, both of them, I

replied. And is that all? He inquired. Small bird
calls up above us. Coyotes squealing far off, & the

hot hissing protest of truck tires on the highway.
Spirit requires a kind of devotion that tears one

away from *one* type of life: *a life of comfort,* I
said. & so one soon learns to undress alone, under

the moonlight. & to rise, solemn, with a good cup
of something hot in the morning &, even then,

Spirit requires a certain loneliness, a solitude—
one that walks parallel with this life, I said. & he

asked: Is it Spirt or *you* that requires solitude?
Soft purring of something in the shaded wood,

louder bewailing higher up, like maybe an owl.
& I answered: it is a road uncommon, & one is

called to walk it, no matter the hour, & that is
the contour of it & I can't explain it further, but

Spirit is the confessor waiting for me there. & it
isn't hiding or dancing like a gypsy & it doesn't

tell me what it is. & it is like a silent attendant,
an accompaniment. And he asked me, *how do you*

know it is Spirit? Loud rustling in the leaves now,
the whole sky an interbella, a flotilla of stars. &

fires, far off, their smoke rising like dead, flat flowers—
the whole world's violence suddenly wrathful, so

traumatic. & the faces of the wounded, the alone,
cinematic; & seeming to undulate & fail in the pine trees

so that above him I could see the true & the untrue
oscillating there, like a distraught heat-lightening.

& then, over the tops of large rocks, every face I'd ever
loved & held close to me for comfort, for joy, for life.

&, over the woodland dingle, small triennial stars—
hovering over wet shrubs, like crystalline phantoms.

Ghost-like, mourning in their absences even, & wet.
Shimmering wet like empty faces across light.

I know it is Spirit, I answered him, because it has
my face. & it is a flute call I must follow alone—

until all this conception, all this daydreaming & this
instruction with my own light, my hunger, is done.

Chasing Names on Nameless Water

—after Robert Hass

& other riddles, he joked with me, cutting fruit
& spreading the jam over the cut wheat. The seeds

peppering the jam. & do you believe in magic?
he inquired. You, who's spending all these hours

writing your verse? & me: magic is spirit's play
of form into formlessness & back, I answered,

& when I write, I apprentice to it, I added. & he
became distracted—polished his old black boots

with the left-over tea in his cup—& returned to
his inquiry. Language fails, though, just at the

point where what you call Spirit arrives, *yes*?
& me, yes, it is a wordlessness that sobers, yes.

& it's a silence that demands attentiveness to it.
& that *is* the magic of it: this activity that stops.

& all I know of the hyperactive hands & the ink pen
is the recognition that we're chasing after something

nameless on a nameless water. & it's nomadic . . .
& the body's made of so much water we're

drunk on it, at most points in our life, & that's
no crime, I said to him while he chiseled out

a scrawled face on the over-dry earth & applied
a kind of hieroglyphics to it so I couldn't read it.

& the violence we do to one another is just the maimed
effort to find a God inside a density of skin that resists it,

this God that is a latent absoluteness in us. & so
we must destroy all the skin on it just to find it,

& it is because we are lost in the crying naked need
of spirit. & the cry consumes us until we cleanse it.

&, because the blood-water in us is so nomadic,
we conclude the cells in us are a *company of words,*

but cells are just permeable, borderless aeons, I
said to him. & he nodded, while yawning at me,

& I can't find my way through the web I've
created with my *own* pen. & he said, *yes,* we make

the web that holds us for a calendar's folly—
& then we disappear into it, like a drunken fruit fly,

& that's the aim, isn't it, in the end? Violins
now playing in the cherry orchard for a wedding—

& the bride & groom, young as two apricots,
stepping forward into one of the webs that is

a celebratory name on a nameless water that is
called *a wedding.* & he to me: nuptials prep us

for the outcome of the poem of the self, which
is an emptiness; it's a wordlessness on a page; or,

as you like to say—in the title poem of your
latest poetry collection—the chasing of names

on a nameless water. & it's true, we follow the violin's
timbre just like names flying over nameless water—

& the practice is to let go of all the sounds, the
names on a nameless water we feel to think

to know. & I think I felt what he was talking
about—when I heard the bees in the orchard

leave the honey combs suddenly, like I don't
quite understand it yet. & the sounds they made. Yes.

Epilogue ('Round This Lover's Ring So Eternal)

—For A, of course

We are children of chance; she whispers to me.
And we are woven into your prologue

and your epilogue. This epilogue is for you:
Let me explain for you: I was just a traveling actress,

suspended in a circus. I'd do the wire dances:
(look at me on a wire, doing the pas ciseaux,

the revoltade, the glissade, the promenade.
My hair up in a lemon bun for you; my toe

shoes like flames.) I was dispatched for you
because the Irish remains of your body

will lose consciousness one day, and all that
will remain will be the wire . . . a torrent to life . . .

beyond happiness . . . this intensity . . . And we will
see the body path to divinity together, she said

to me. Wear my shoes until their heels are flames
of glory, until we become a gesture that vanishes,

Bride and Groom; gold-ringed light. And we, too,
will remain available until we come back in our

vaporous shoes, in our tutus; in our eyes that see
the Eternal in the salt water, in the dark, in sex,

and in those prayers we pray that send us
beyond the children of time—where the

almond blossoms are the passion play
of the light most glad of all. We'll meet—

as we said we would—by the stage door,
the latch not quite unlocked until we love

it open; inexpressibly, precisely; and we'll
walk in the beautiful forms that we have

asked of ourselves to inhabit here; and
we'll find one another; again and again;

shoeless wanderers stopping for the other to
bend low and slip the slipper on the other—

your face and body so linked with mine;
and we will dance with that rebellious

angel-gazer in us with its eyes wide open while
the veiled, white almond blossoms shower

down all over us as we stroll every single aisle of it—
wedded, bonded, encircled, haloed, ringed,

interwoven, sewn, blended in this life we were
meant to live together, like two almond blossom

storms converging until the end of the story
swallows the very pit at the beginning of it . . .

and so on and on and on . . . and isn't
that exactly what we vowed to one another

so long ago before the trees were even
planted, 'round this lover's ring so eternal?

Mary Magdalene Utters Words of Wisdom

By the hard rocks where the well was, they'd gathered;
the morning sun, rising boisterous, ecclesiastic

over the tortured mountain rock. It would be hot today.
Mathew & Judas stood there, beside her, robed, sandaled.

She said, "I've been with the Master; he is well." Then:
"The wickedness of each day is sufficient; it's what marks us

with the candid will to survive, until we thrive . . . and we'll thrive
in that light that has no diocese to it—except that it is

beyond *these* garments." The men stood silent, listened.
And then she said: "Workers *deserve* their food. We who work

against the ignorance that binds and ties us to ourselves—
to that greed that will not let us pass the door of light in us—

will earn, and be fulfilled in that other food that has no false
apostolicity to it. And it is earned only by that careful choosing

that disrobes one's self from enormity. The work is small:
it passes us through only the *smallest place:* and it has no trust

of enormity, which is the struggle of the falsified eyes, always:
and it always blocks the beginning of the way. Mathew & Judas

sipped water from cups, sat quietly on the red side of the well,
listened further. Mary then said: "Disciples resemble their

teachers: they learn from their wisdom, and also their folly,
and then they must find their own way home, through the

ignoble false light that blocks even the teacher, and then
the light pours down. And when the truth-light pours down

(upon us) we are drowned but emerge victorious,
and it will take standing in that place of reach, when we strip

ourselves of garments, that Spirit is disclosed. And then she said,
"The Master has told us just this: One who does not stand

in the darkness cannot see the light. And those who come
after us will dwell in that unwashed riddle, and many

will die. It is best that we try to drink from that well
that has no water in it, but just vision. And if we can

just *drink the vision,* we will see the birth of a new soul
into the world. And then we will have done our work."

Listening to Astral Weeks & Emailing Russell Thorburn

& Van Morrison is wailing about the fragile dancer
& telling her
to spread her ballerina wings
for if she doesn't, the wind, the wild air,
will simply whisk her away
where she will then become glued, like seal wax,
to the rippling olive-tinted water
wiggling just behind a factory where they bake soap
& sell it to hotel chains outside the city,
& so she'd be stolen down stream and written
into another's love song, the ballerina.
& the strings on Ballerina tell us just a bit about a song,
especially that it is an unfixed shape, a dancer
on a trapeze wire. & the I withdraws into beauty,
it has to surrender to it
because the trace of the shape of the ballerina
is liminal, it's barely there,
& it's so transient that it could fall into another's
pocket, into another's love ballades poem,

& so Morrison, right there in the studio, grabs it,
the song & not the ballerina
because she's already gone, is just a trace
of herself as Levinas would say—she's emanation—
& she's just a little eyelash hair on my paper,
& so I email Russ just to tell him
I've found it right here, the eyelash, the emanation,
& I put it on this poem, for him.

Under Water

We are swimming in a pond, somewhere
off a campsite, (it might have been out west

where the chilled water would refresh us,
the pine trees & sloped ridges surrounding us

like conifer castles.) & I dive in, go deep
to search the gravel stone & murky bottom

while you float on top. & if I could pare down
gravity just enough, so I could pull you

down underwater w/ me, the both of us
sudden gilled fishes, caudal tails flickering

like wet matches lit by flame so that the
understory of the pond's arboretum could

be cathedral light, then down there, we'd
find all our other hidden lives, their agile

bodies eager & waiting for us to discover
them, their blossom hands & tubular fingers

reaching out to greet us, all our varied souls,
oh mirror of water, reveal us to ourselves.

Under God (The Angels Discuss Our Music)

The angels laid around on sofas, read poetry, listened to music,
talked of the key difference between the Rolling Stones

and the Beatles, and agreed it was just a matter of focus—
that John, Paul, George and Ringo were more about the space

inside a bright melody, and that *in the light,* we were still consolable,
whereas the Stones were juke joint—just cigarettes and Lucifer

and after-hours blues, whereas say, someone like Leonard Cohen
had blended his ardor with lust and with love's articulate torment,

and thus would reside with them, here in their golden parlor
forever, like one of them, a literary music box, a true composer

lost inextricably in music's metaphysical form. And then some
of the angels caressed their larger wings as if they were preparing

for fermentation, for that vibration that enlightened ones *master,*
en route to their inner soul's inebriation into the truly divine—

whereas the other angels, those of the lesser known solitudes, were but
ideas of feelings, incomplete songs, and so they wailed and sobbed

so that all of us below them—*you*—could hear their lamenting,
and one of the angels, whose heart had burst open like a torn fruit,

argued that Dylan, soon to be among them, had combined
literary seeing with all forms of vocalization—he was a magpie—

and thus would achieve a kind of exalted grace, no doubt
embarrassing for him, in the same way a mockingbird, if caught,

goes silent as a still river for a while until it can imitate only
a wordlessness, which in the end would be infinite domain—

a kind of enlightenment meant only for those special ones
who eschew glory for the endpoint of genius, which is artistic

light—the full erasure of any referent point of a self.
And one argued that Van Morrison, that Irish rogue whose

balding head resembled a fresh cantaloupe, would reside here
because he'd allowed a vaguely felt light beside his left temple

to make a love *passionate*—like a spinning ballerina—and thus
he too could transcend, could join them here eating raspberries

while the melodies of the spheres vibrated on, in agreeable tones.
And one of the angels, winged like a bird, spoke of Joni Mitchell,

that her voice rivaled a thrush or a heralding loon, and so she
too should arrive here following the silencing of her virtuoso;

such could be the advancement of this upward, Heavenly choir.
And God, above all this, so incalculable and so inscrutable—

so complicated in allusive illusion, liminal like an oracle spent
with fate—became the memory of other spaces, concerts, tunes—

just a cistern where all the music of human feelings became
whole tree branches of doves expressing their images of insight

and time; and the angels below God could track only how he fell
into disarray as he was lifting the rags of his music into that

mustard glow that is the farthest outreach of Heaven, the last throes
of perception, where ecstasy and holy experiences abide.

And one angel, thick with pomegranate, said that God was being
imitated by Tom Waits; he was masquerading in rags and tatters.

And that Waits would soon be Heaven's janitor, just a bum
at the margins, a jester for God whose gentle hands rested on him.

Another angel, wrapped in eulophiella orchids—purple, white—
offered Patti Smith up, that Easter Angel whose voice startles, softens,

clings like a ringlet of flowers to the Corinthian columns, the ancient
of days, the collapsed stone altars crumbled on Heaven's paths.

And a last angel, himself a finality in the shape of a soap box,
offered Paul Simon up, for writing songs that eavesdrop on love.

And the other angels, gathered there, sang in chorus at a lamppost,
like two-hearted singers in a barbershop quartet—for God.

And God maintained a lit-up duration composed of realization
and action, just a passage into dimension. And like a lone fallen star

perpetuating the tensions of time, of its vast audible sound
which goes on and on in our dreams, on our record players,

and in the clubs we love in like entwined soul-light, God listened
to the music our hearts were giving back to him, like shaped time.

Notes

The poem "Mizocz Ghetto, October 1942" refers to the horrific slaughter of a group of Jewish women and children in the Mizocz Ghetto during World War II—which was Eastern Poland at that time, and is now part of Western Ukraine.

"The Algiers Motel Incident, 1967 & Everything Else Thereafter Till Now" references the 1967 murder of innocent civilians at the now demolished Algiers Motel during the summer of 1967 riots in Detroit.

The poem "First Kiss" is dedicated to Sharon.

The final line of the poem, "Glory & Shame Cannot Be Separated from Each Other" is borrowed from Sandra Cisneros's short story collection, *Woman Hollering Creek*.

The poem "St. William of the Artists Studio" is dedicated to Bill Johnson.

The poem "The Angel of Let Me Remember My Name" is dedicated to Anita.

The poem "J, an Elegy in 20 lines" is for J. May she dwell in peace.

The poem "An Elegy for Robert Wachler" is dedicated to Rob and Judy Wachler.

The poem "Under Water" is inspired by Tim Marshall's photograph, which is represented on the cover of this book.

About the Author

Ken Meisel is a poet and psychotherapist from the Detroit area. He is a 2012 Kresge Arts Literary Fellow, Pushcart Prize nominee, Best of the Net nominee, winner of the Liakoura Prize, and author of nine poetry collections.

His recent books include *The Light Most Glad of All* (Kelsay Books, 2023), *Studies Inside the Consent of a Distance* (Kelsay Books, 2022), and *Our Common Souls: New & Selected Poems of Detroit* (Blue Horse Press, 2020). He has had poetry published in over 100 poetry journals including in *Crab Creek Review, I-70 Review, San Pedro River Review, Sheila-Na-Gig, St. Katherine Review, U City Review, Tipton Poetry Journal, Trampoline Magazine, Lake Effect, Wasteland Review,* and *The Glacier.*

www.ingramcontent.com/pod-product-compliance
Lightning Source LLC
Chambersburg PA
CBHW022013160426
43197CB00007B/416